DRESSAGE
SCHOOL

Britta Schöffmann

DRESSAGE
SCHOOL

A SOURCEBOOK
OF MOVEMENTS AND TIPS
DEMONSTRATED BY
OLYMPIAN ISABELL WERTH

Translated by Reina Abelshauser

TRAFALGAR SQUARE
North Pomfret, Vermont

First published in the United States of America in 2009 by
Trafalgar Square Books
North Pomfret, Vermont 05053

Printed in China

Originally published in the German language as *Lektinonen Richtig Reiten* by Franckh-Kosmos Verlags-GmbH & Co. KG, Stuttgart, Germany, 2005.

Copyright © 2005 Franckh-Kosmos Verlags-GmbH & Co. KG, Stuttgart
English translation © 2009 Trafalgar Square Books

Disclaimer of Liability
The authors and publisher shall have neither liability nor responsibility to any person or entity with respect to any loss or damage caused or alleged to be caused directly or indirectly by the information contained in this book. While the book is as accurate as the authors can make it, there may be errors, omissions, and inaccuracies.

Library of Congress Cataloging-in-Publication Data
Schoffmann, Britta.
  [Lektinonen Richtig Reiten. English]
  Dressage school : a sourcebook of movements and tips demonstrated by olympian Isabell Werth / Britta Schoffmann ; translated by Reina Abelshauser.
      p. cm.
  "Originally published in the German language as Lektinonen Richtig Reiten by Franckh-Kosmos Verlags-GmbH & Co. KG, Stuttgart, Germany, 2005"--T.p. verso.
  ISBN 978-1-57076-411-0 (jacketed hardback) 1. Dressage. 2. Dressage horses--Training. I. Title.

  SF309.5.S4266 2009

  798.2'3--dc22

                    2008053905

Production: Kristin Raue, Claudia Kupferer
Cover design by Carrie Fradkin
10 9 8 7 6 5 4 3 2 1

AN IMPORTANT NOTE FROM THE PUBLISHER

Britta Schöffmann's *Dressage School* seemed such an infinitely useful book, it made sense to translate it for the thousands of English-speaking dressage riders around the world. However, the book was written and designed as an alphabetical dictionary with its original German audience in mind, so its organization in the English language does not adhere to any particular system. To ensure it remains the handy, easy-to-use reference the author intended it, you will find not only a table of contents listing the movements, school figures, and exercises in the order they actually appear in the book, but also an alphabetical index (see p. ix) for quick-search purposes. In addition, the current topic of discussion is noted at the top of every right-hand page throughout the book.

CONTENTS

Note for the Reader

Please see the Important Note from the Publisher on p. v.

At the end of every movement described in this book, you ll find the "Training Pyramid Factor"—a list marked with stars, which tells you how much the exercise furthers the respective element of the Training Pyramid: * means a little; *** means a lot.

ALPHABETICAL INDEX

FOREWORD

When Britta Schöffmann contacted me, telling me she was
writing another book and asking if I'd be willing to make
myself available as a "riding model," I was happy to say yes.
First of all, I've known Britta for many years—she is a very
good and responsible rider and horse owner. And second, the
concept of this book appealed to me—especially important is
the emphasis on the meaning of the individual dressage movements *within* the overall context of a horse's training. Only the
rider who understands *why* the movements are important and
what their purposes are can build a dressage horse systematically. This applies to both the development of the horse's muscles and the development of his mind.

As riders, we must always be aware of the fact that we can't
train horses using a rigid framework of principles. Every horse
is different, and every horse is an individual. For this reason, we must adjust our training
methods to suit each horse's personality and his particular talents. Something similar can
be said about dressage movements themselves. First of all, a movement or exercise might
appear different depending on the horse performing it, and second, each one may need to
be learned by each individual horse in quite a different manner. What comes easily to one
horse might not to another. As riders, we must develop a "feel" for the exercises that will
best further a particular horse's training. The rider who is unable to do this can potentially
ruin a lot of horses!

This "feel" needs to begin in the horse's basic training: although the three foundation levels
of the Training Pyramid—rhythm, relaxation and suppleness, and contact—should certainly
have priority early in training, the way to achieving them can differ from horse to horse.
While one horse relaxes more quickly when stretching toward the bit with movements such
as serpentines and leg-yields, another might achieve the same goal more easily through
transitions and increasing pace or lengthening stride. When training horses, we must *never*
lose sight of each horse's individuality.

Isabell Werth
Winner of five gold and three silver Olympic medals,
and multiple German, European, and World Championships

PREFACE

Dressage! "Oh, the sport where girls ride in circles," equestrians in other disciplines often joke. The fact that there's much more to dressage than just "riding in circles" is often forgotten, even by those devoted individuals who pursue it tirelessly over many years. In fact, you can often see dressage riders practicing the same movement, the same school figure, over and over again—yet it can be just as apparent they have no real understanding of its purpose.

This is where *Dressage School* enters the picture—it is meant to serve as a practical and easy-to-use reference book that not only explains the "What" of a certain figure, movement, or exercise, but also the "How" and (especially) the "Why." The latter is of particular concern to me because the secret of training any horse eventually lies in the "Why"—regardless if you ride dressage, jump, or pursue a Western discipline. What's the purpose of a simple change of lead? Why ride a volte? Because it's required in a dressage test? Certainly not—or at least, that's not the *only* reason why you use it. Without understanding this and the interconnectedness between movements, without being able to put each movement in the context of the Training Pyramid, a rider can't improve her riding or her horse's conditioning, carriage, and obedience.

For example, instead of going out and riding a dozen failing attempts at flying lead changes, it helps to know beforehand that a flying change will only be successful if the horse can "jump through" well in the canter. And, the latter can only occur by improving the horse's relaxation and suppleness, and increasing his "carrying power." So instead of practicing in a way that almost guarantees a struggle with your horse, you are better off working systematically on the canter itself. And this, in turn, can only be done by using other movements and exercises, and understanding *their* purpose in training. Dressage movements were developed and have evolved over time and through centuries' of riders' experience. Their goal is to provide the ultimate progressive physical training for the horse.

Britta Schöffmann

A lovely turn to the right.

TURNING
Initiating a turn with the horse evenly flexed and bent, while maintaining the same tempo, in order to change direction or ride the line on a circle.

HOW IT'S SUPPOSED TO LOOK Many a rider might be thinking, "Turning can't be that difficult!" Just pull a little bit on the inside rein and the horse turns in no time—right? Theoretically, this is true to some extent, and sometimes might even work. However, if done this way, a turn will rarely look correct. Turning only becomes beautiful and correct when it's done completely smoothly on a more or less gently curved line with contact, tempo, and rhythm remaining the same, and the aids invisible. During the entire turn, the horse is supposed to bend evenly around the rider's inside leg, exhibiting *lateral bend* (see p. 76), while taking up more of his weight on his inside *hind* leg. This unburdens the horse's inside *front* leg, a process that not only keeps the horse's rhythm pure in the turn but also prevents—especially at the trot and canter—wear and tear on the joints, which contributes to keeping the horse sound. The latter, especially, should be the reason for every rider to work on turning correctly. After all, in any riding session you turn countless times—whether on a trail ride, in the dressage ring, or in the jumping arena.

When turning, the horse bends around the longitudinal axis of his body.

MOST COMMON MISTAKES The Horse: evades through his outside shoulder; drifts sideways; is on the forehand; tilts his head at the poll; does not stay on the arc of the circle. **The Rider:** "pulls" the horse around; turns only using one rein.

CORRECT AIDS The key for executing a good turn lies in the correct orchestration of all aids, as in all exercises and movements. Begin with a half-halt on the outside rein in order to gain the horse's attention, then shorten the inside rein enough to slightly flex the horse to the inside. Your inside leg drives (the horse's inside hind leg) forward at the girth, and your outside leg is positioned slightly behind the girth, keeping the haunches under control and bending

the horse around your inside leg. At the moment of turning, increase the inside rein aid a bit, yielding slightly with the outside rein.

However, be careful not to "throw the rein away" as this will cause the horse to run "through" his outside shoulder. The outside rein must keep enough contact to set a boundary for the horse's outside shoulder, and "give" just enough to allow the horse to stretch the muscles on the outside of his neck and prevent him from tilting his head at the poll. Your outside rein and outside leg take on the role of the arena fence or wall, so to speak, from which a horse would turn on his own. (If the horse still evades through his outside shoulder, most of the time it helps to counterflex him temporarily.) Ultimately, a horse that is trained correctly actually turns from the outside rein, while the inside rein only provides the flexion.

The better you are able to concentrate on your aids, the more precisely you will be able to turn your horse at any gait, using only the slightest of aids.

GOAL OF THE MOVEMENT Apart from being the tool used for changing rein or riding a circle, every turn that's executed cleanly and neatly also has the effect of bending the horse around the rider's inside leg for a moment, causing him to step more underneath the center of his mass with his inside hind leg, thus taking up more weight. The muscles on the inside of his body momentarily shorten while the ones on the outside stretch—an unspectacular, yet effective, gymnastic exercise.

FAST FACTS Basic exercise; improves lateral mobility.

PYRAMID FACTOR Rhythm*, relaxation/suppleness*, contact**, impulsion**, straightness**, collection**.

FIGURE EIGHT

Connecting two voltes or circles to form an exercise ridden as one piece to resemble a figure eight.

HOW IT'S SUPPOSED TO LOOK

If, for example, you take the arena as a whole and at "X" volte (p. 171)—or circle (p. 179)—left, then when you again cross "X," begin a circle to the right, you will complete a figure eight. It's supposed to be ridden fluidly, with both circles equal in size. At the intersection point after completing the first volte, straighten the horse for about one horse's length, and only then enter the second part of the figure eight. This creates two circles opposing each other, which should match precisely.

MOST COMMON MISTAKES

The Horse: is tight in the neck; allows his haunches to fall out on the circle(s); goes against the hand when changing flexion and bend.
The Rider: plans circles poorly; makes size of circles unequal; rides circles misshapen; "pulls" horse around the turns.

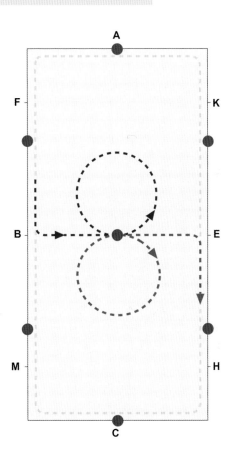

The two voltes that make up a figure eight must match perfectly—in form and size.

CORRECT AIDS If you are able to perform correct circles or voltes, riding a precise figure eight is merely a matter of concentration. Many riders make the mistake of hurrying back to the intersection point after they ride the first half of the first circle—essentially cutting off the second half of the circle, instead of completing it roundly and properly before thinking about beginning the new one.

To initiate the figure eight: slightly shorten the inside rein, flex the horse slightly to the inside, and keep the inside leg at the girth while positioning the outside leg behind the girth, bending the horse around the inside leg. At the end of the first circle, briefly straighten the horse on the line where you "began" the figure eight, then immediately enter the second circle on the other rein.

GOAL OF THE MOVEMENT When performing a figure eight in a dressage test, you inform the judges about your ability to influence your horse and also about the horse's suppleness on both sides. When schooling, riding figure eights provides a great opportunity to further and improve this very suppleness—that is, lateral bend—both to the right and the left, especially if you ride several figure eights in a row. However, *do not* make the circles too small, as this puts too much stress on the horse's ligaments and joints.

Figure eights are best ridden at the trot, but you can also ride them at the canter, using either a simple change (p. 41) or a flying change (p. 45) of lead when changing direction.

FAST FACTS Basic exercise; suitable for the end of the warm-up, the work phase, and the cool-down; can be ridden at both a working and collected gait (see pp. 15 and 165).

PYRAMID FACTOR Rhythm*, relaxation/suppleness***, contact**, impulsion*, straightness**, collection*.

CANTER DEPART
The transition from the halt, walk, or trot into the canter.

HOW IT'S SUPPOSED TO LOOK The canter depart should occur in balance and spontaneously; that is, promptly following the rider's aids with contact remaining quiet and consistent, and immediately resulting in the clear three-beat rhythm of a proper canter stride on the required lead. The horse's body should remain "straight" on the line of travel, whether on a line or the arc of a curve.

How is this done? The answer is quite simple: the strike-off on a straight line—on the short or long side of the arena—occurs with a slight inside flexion (at the poll) *without* lateral bend (p. 76), and the strike-off on a curved line—such as when riding on a circle—occurs *with* lateral bend, according to the line of travel. "Straightening" a horse does not mean making him straight like a railroad tie. Instead it means that he places his hind feet into or beyond the tracks of his front feet, not to the side of them. So, during the strike-off into the canter, the horse's leading hind leg "jumps" directly underneath his center of gravity, and all four legs step straight along the line of travel.

MOST COMMON MISTAKES The Horse: requires multiple attempts before cantering; takes the incorrect lead (counter-canter instead of "true" canter and vice versa); is against the rider's hand; has a tight neck; is on the forehand; breaks into the trot (when riding a walk-canter transition); has a high croup; is crooked; is against the rider's legs; kicks out. **The Rider:** uses too much spur and causes kicking out; allows her upper body to fall forward (attempting to create momentum for the canter depart).

CORRECT AIDS The aids for the canter depart are identical whether you depart from the halt, walk, or trot. The difference lies in the level of difficulty. The canter depart from the halt and walk requires a certain amount of collection and a higher degree of "straightness." This is because the transition is from a halt or movement *without* impulsion into a gait *with* impulsion. This requires more strength from the hindquarters as well as increased horse-and-rider coordination.

The canter depart itself is done as follows: slightly flex the horse in the poll to the inside, give a half-halt on the outside rein to tell the horse that a new task is at hand. At the same time, move your outside leg behind the girth, and with the inside calf give a forward-driving aid by applying brief and distinct pressure. At the moment when the horse responds and wants to strike-off, move your inside hand slightly forward. This "giving" action is particularly important because the horse begins the canter with his inside hind leg, which means that this leg comes more forward and under his body, bearing his weight for a brief moment—the prerequisite for the change from one gait into another. When a rider blocks this process by having a too tight inside rein, the horse will barely be able to strike-off on the correct lead. In such a situation, a horse that tends to take a strong contact often "takes" the rein himself by objecting with his head, while a horse that tends to take a lighter contact will "collapse" backward with his head behind the vertical in order to find the necessary space to complete the canter depart.

In order to make the canter depart fluid and available to you at any time, it's enormously important that you correctly organize the leg, hand, and seat (weight/back) aids. Part of this correct orchestration of aids is an even application of your leg and seat aids. This means that the outside leg behind the girth mustn't squeeze, since the horse might interpret it as a lateral driving aid and evade sideways with his haunches. Your outside leg should instead lie quite loosely on the horse and, at the most, *prevent* the horse from evading sideways to the outside, while the inside leg gives the forward impulse for the depart.

If the horse strikes off on the wrong lead—a common problem—it is often caused by a rider's failing to focus on "fine-tuning" all the necessary aids. But, it is also caused by a lack of "straightness" in the horse's body. When this is the issue, it helps to initially school the canter depart on bending lines, either in the corners of the arena or on a circle. When the horse's inside hind leg is already placed a bit more under the center of his body mass, and bend and flexion have already been established—at least, when the turn has been ridden correctly—most horses find it easier to obtain the correct lead. And, since riding on bending lines furthers the horse's "straightness," it most often is only a matter of time until the canter depart will work on straight lines, too, without any problems.

It doesn't help to swing your upper body forward and back to establish momentum, as many riders do to encourage the strike-off into the canter. A rider might in fact swing beautifully with his body—but he will not be able to establish momentum. Instead, he will usually achieve the opposite: at the moment he falls forward, he lightens his seat, and combined with the half-halt and one leg positioned behind the girth, almost gives the aid for the rein-back! Since his inside leg is driving the horse forward at the same time, the confused horse will react with incomprehension, possibly thinking: "What am I supposed to do? Do I canter forward or step backward?" Aids must always be clear—without ambiguity.

The canter depart should always look spontaneous.

GOAL OF THE MOVEMENT The canter depart is mainly an end in itself: to transition into the canter from another gait. However, especially in combination with transitions into slower gaits, it can also help improve contact and the horse's relaxation and suppleness.

FAST FACTS Basic exercise; schools coordination skills.

PYRAMID FACTOR Rhythm*, relaxation/suppleness***, contact***, impulsion**, straightness**, collection*.

Only when leg, hand, and seat aids are orchestrated correctly will the horse perform a straight strike-off into the canter.

WALKING OFF
Setting the horse in motion from the halt into the walk.

HOW IT'S SUPPOSED TO LOOK Walking off from the halt should always occur spontaneously and immediately from the slightest possible aids. Ideally, the horse walks on perfectly straight and seemingly on his own, remaining quietly on the aids. When walking off, the horse should immediately reach for the contact, with the first stride rhythmical and with correct tempo.

MOST COMMON MISTAKES The Horse: delays motion; exhibits rhythm faults; is strung out; wanders. **The Rider:** uses too strong, too visible aids (pounding leg aids, overuse of spurs).

CORRECT AIDS In order for the horse to walk on correctly, he must respond well to your leg. This means that when you apply even, brief calf pressure, he immediately responds by moving forward. If you want him to walk from the halt, you must create this pressure from both calves, while giving a half-halt and slightly yielding with both hands. The better a horse reacts to the leg aids, the better the initial walk steps usually are. When the horse remains standing as if glued to the ground, or if he sluggishly responds to your driving aids only after you repeatedly ask, you must not hesitate to give a stronger tap with your calves.

It's crucial to also *allow* the horse to go forward at that very moment, whether or not he is perfectly on the aids. After he

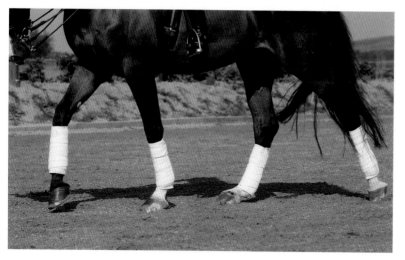

Even the first step after walking off should be in a clear four-beat rhythm.

understands this go-forward cue, it will usually be enough to give a gentle squeeze with your calves, and he will respond by moving on immediately. However, if, after giving the stronger leg aid, you restrain the horse by moving your hands backward, he will definitely be confused. So, remember to yield your hands forward, thus rewarding the horse for going forward. Only then will the horse understand what you really want.

If you have problems with him moving off "straight," use this little trick: focus your eyes on an object or point ahead of you and ride exactly toward it. This automatically helps you distribute your aids more evenly. When practicing this, it's helpful to walk toward a mirror in the ring as it allows you to develop a feel for a straight line and the uniform, equal use of your legs.

GOAL OF THE MOVEMENT The horse not only sets himself in motion, he also activates his "engine"—the hindquarters—in order to move forward. For this reason, walking off is always a great, yet simple exercise to strengthen the muscles in the hindquarters.

FAST FACTS Basic exercise.

PYRAMID FACTOR Rhythm, relaxation/suppleness, contact, impulsion, straightness, collection.

TROTTING OFF
The transition from the halt or walk into the trot.

HOW IT'S SUPPOSED TO LOOK Just as when walking off, trotting off should also be smooth and occur spontaneously from the slightest of aids. And, when riding a halt-trot transition, the *very first* stride should be a trot stride. Trotting off from the walk must be prompt, leading from the clear four-beat walk rhythm into the two-beat trot rhythm. The horse should be evenly on the aids and impulsion for the transition should come from his hindquarters. The more balanced and aligned a horse, is the better the walk-trot transition will be.

MOST COMMON MISTAKES The Horse: (from the halt) transition is not immediate; wanders; walks prior to trotting; (from the walk) jigs in the transition; is against the rider's hand. **The Rider:** uses too strong, too visible aids.

Precise aids

Every aid should be applied clearly and precisely so the horse responds to it, or a combination of aids, immediately and promptly. When he has learned this, he will be ready to respond to finer and lighter aids in the future.

CORRECT AIDS Although this exercise might seem simple, it can be tricky. In a dressage test, the difficulty begins after the first salute (p. 51), where the rider is often required to transition from the halt into a "working" or "collected trot" (pp. 15 and 165). It could be said that the salute and this first transition are a rider's "signature," so to speak, setting the tone for the whole test. When a rider has problems at this point, she must make up for it in the following movements in order to still get a decent score. If, on the other hand, the transition into the trot is textbook—that is, it's spontaneous, perfectly straight, and with the horse securely on the aids—you have the first good mark securely under your belt.

For a halt-trot transition, give a half-halt to briefly prepare the horse, as always when initiating a new movement. This tells the horse, "Pay attention, something is going to happen." In order to prevent the horse from getting excited, trot on immediately. For this transition, brace your back slightly (sit up a little more), give an evenly distributed, gentle forward cue with your legs while at the same moment slightly "giving" the hands forward. "Slightly" doesn't mean throw the reins away—this causes you to lose the contact, which confuses the horse. Give only as much as necessary for the horse to stretch forward into your hands while he converts forward impulsion from his hind legs into movement.

The aids for the walk-trot transition are generally identical as those for halt-trot. However, usually it's enough to give a somewhat quieter cue with the legs since the horse is already moving. To prevent loss of rhythm, falling onto the forehand, or jigging, it's crucial to orchestrate your driving leg aids with your restraining and yielding rein aids. If a horse tends to lean too much on a rider's hands during the trot transition when the driving aids are insufficient, he will appear "tipped" onto his forehand. It helps to drive this horse more actively toward the hands while restraining with the reins a little longer. You proceed differently with a horse that habitually comes behind the bit and leg, and therefore tends to jig before trotting off.

Concentration

A condition for the success of each lesson and each exercise is concentration—on the part of both the rider and the horse. Ten minutes concentrated work will accomplish more than an hour's ride with little or no purpose.

In this case, you need to increase the driving aids and combine them with lighter rein aids that encourage the horse to stretch his neck forward.

GOAL OF THE MOVEMENT One of the purposes of trotting off is, of course, to transition to the trot from the halt or walk. But there's more to it, especially when riding halt-trot transitions. Here, impulsion coming from the muscles in the hindquarters needs to be much stronger than when riding a walk-trot transition. This larger transmission of energy toward the horse's mouth, via his back, causes the horse to stretch more into the rider's hand, which is what you want. For this reason, halt-trot transitions are a very good exercise to improve contact, strengthen the muscles in the hindquarters, improve thrust, and develop "carrying power" later on.

FAST FACTS Basic exercise; teaches coordination and promotes body strength.

When trotting off, the rider should maintain the rhythm of the gait, and contact as shown.

PYRAMID FACTOR Rhythm*, relaxation/suppleness**, contact***, impulsion**, straightness*, collection**.

WORKING PIROUETTE

An exercise to prepare for the canter pirouette. The horse "lifts" his forehand on a quarter turn around the hindquarters while the hindquarters are allowed to follow the bending line of a small circle.

HOW IT'S SUPPOSED TO LOOK During a working pirouette, the horse must maintain the canter stride with impulsion and in a clear three-beat rhythm while treading a small circle or bending line with his hind feet and "lifting" his forehand in a quarter turn around them. He should be flexed in the poll to the inside and bent around the rider's inside leg as he gradually bears more weight on his hind legs, lowers his hindquarters, and increases flexion in his haunches.

The prerequisite for the working pirouette is a very collected canter—the horse should be able to canter for two or three strides almost "on the spot" without losing rhythm and impulsion.

MOST COMMON MISTAKES The Horse: is against (not yielding to) the rider's inside leg; is against the hands; is tight in the neck; displays insufficient impulsion from behind; displays insufficient collection; has rhythm that is too fast, too slow, or inconsistent; evades through the outside shoulder; allows his hindquarters to drift to the outside.

CORRECT AIDS Working pirouettes are commonly developed from "decreasing the circle" (p. 181). You can start the movement on other lines—for example, the half-volte or from the quarterline toward the wall of the arena (p. 68)—however, decreasing the circle is suitable because it already requires the horse to increase the flexion in his

In the working pirouette, the horse learns to take up more of his weight with his hindquarters.

haunches and so prepare to bear more weight on them. When planning the working pirouette, it is helpful to alternately decrease the circle in a "travers-like" manner, and increase it in a "shoulder-in-like" manner, allowing you to gain control over both the horse's hindquarters and shoulders (this also helps when you practice true canter pirouettes later on—see p. 99).

To decrease the circle in a travers-like manner, gather the horse with hal[f] halts, increase the weight on your inside seat bone, keep your inside leg the girth to maintain the canter and your outside leg behind the girth to maintain the bend. Shorten your inside rein slightly to flex the horse wh giving with the outside rein to allow for it. Your inside leg and outside r keep the horse on the desired line of travel.

To increase the circle in a shoulder-in-like manner, position your inside slightly behind the girth to drive the horse forward and sideways, positioning the hindquarters to the outside and the forehand to the inside.

You should be able to alternate between travers and shoulder-in decreases and increases before you attempt a working pirouette.

GOAL OF THE MOVEMENT Working pirouettes are a preliminary exercise for the canter pirouettes in later training. They allow you to gradually develop more flexion in your horse's haunches, as well as his strength and coordination. They improve the canter stride and further "straightness."

FAST FACTS Collected exercise used in the work phase, for advanced riders and horses; promotes coordination and carrying power.

PYRAMID FACTOR Rhythm**, relaxation/suppleness*, contact*, impulsion**, straightness**, collection***.

WORKING GAITS
A pace (trot or canter) that is energetic yet calm, where the horse's hind hooves touch the ground right in or slightly ahead of the front hooves' prints—the length of stride is between that of the collected and medium paces.

HOW IT'S SUPPOSED TO LOOK Regardless of which working gait you are riding, it must look "fresh," be rhythmically pure, and the horse must be engaged. At first glance, variations within a gait seem to have something in common with speed—the working canter being the "medium" speed, so to speak. However, this is only true to a certain extent. When moving from a collected to a working to an extended pace, the horse does not speed up but makes each stride of the trot or canter *longer*. This is how you cover the distance between two points more quickly; thus, riding at a collected pace between A and C takes longer than riding the same distance at an extended pace. This alteration in the length of strides requires the horse's hindquarters to shift from "carrying power" to "pushing power." When riding at a working gait, carrying and pushing power are almost equal. For this reason, working gaits are suitable for younger horses or horses with little training, and are therefore required in Young Horse Tests, as well as Training and First Level dressage tests (Preliminary and Novice in the UK).

MOST COMMON MISTAKES The Horse: is too dull; is too hurried; exhibits an uneven rhythm; is on the forehand.

CORRECT AIDS In order to ride an appropriate working gait, the rider really only has to find—through feel—the tempo that's natural for the horse, and make it readily available under saddle. If you remember to always also include engagement and "freshness," the working gait will be acceptable most of the time. There are horses, however, that naturally, or from incorrect training, drag their feet. Instead of lifting their legs energetically and with spring, they move lazily and without enthusiasm—they're thinking, "Better not overexert myself!" When this happens, respond by increasing the driving aids, invigorating the horse by giving brief forward impulses with your legs. Only this way can you prevent the next mistake— falling onto the forehand. A horse that sluggishly drags his feet through the arena footing is not able to move forward with a "swinging" back. Being "forward," together with a swinging back, enables the horse to "step" into the rider's hands, which creates the necessary contact—the most important prerequisite for managing other movements successfully as well as the horse's entire physical development.

GOAL OF THE MOVEMENT The working pace is ridden at the tempo closest to the horse's natural paces in all three basic gaits, and therefore, initially, requires the least amount of work from the horse. For this reason, it's suitable for the warm-up phase, for young horses, and also for horses whose riders are not yet familiar with the aiding that creates more flexion in the haunches and ultimately collection. Riding in a working gait also furthers the horse's relaxation, suppleness, and the natural energy of his movements, and should therefore always be a component in the training of upper-level horses, as well.

FAST FACTS Basic exercise; required at Training and First Level dressage tests (Preliminary and Novice in the UK) as well as in Young Horse Tests; loosens up the horse; builds endurance and, to a certain degree, "pushing power."

PYRAMID FACTOR Rhythm**, relaxation/suppleness***, contact***, impulsion***, straightness**, collection.

In the working canter, the horse is "jumping through" with his hind legs far underneath his body.

WORKING TROT

A pace within the trot gait that encourages the horse's hind hooves to touch the ground slightly ahead of the front hooves—a length of stride between that of the collected and medium paces—as can be seen by the horse's hoofprints.

HOW IT'S SUPPOSED TO LOOK The working trot must be active, rhythmically pure, and ridden energetically forward with an "uphill" appearance. Furthermore, the horse must have a secure and even contact with the bit and respond to the slightest aids.

MOST COMMON MISTAKES The Horse: is too dull; is too hurried; exhibits uneven rhythm; is on the forehand; is not securely on the aids.

CORRECT AIDS In order to be able to ride an even, "fresh," and lively working trot, the back of the horse must be "swinging." In order to achieve this, you must be able to sit well balanced and finely orchestrate the interplay between your legs, seat, and hands. Only when you are able to do this can you ride an expressive working trot.

While both legs "drive" the horse forward, keep an upright seat and "intercept" the horse's impulsion coming from behind, then let it out in the front by (slightly) yielding both hands. Your driving aids "ask" the horse's hind legs to swing through underneath his body, while your simultaneous interception of this impulsion prevents the horse's forehand from "crashing" downward. Yielding the hands at the right moment allows the desired "forward-upward" movement to unfold—and thus the working trot gains expression. Yielding *does not* mean "throwing the reins away." Many riders make the mistake of repeatedly pushing the hands so far forward, so suddenly, that the horse becomes insecure about the contact. Yielding only means to *relax* your fists and lower arms, "letting them breathe," so to speak. The few millimeters or centimeters of space this action creates allows the horse to stretch as necessary. A more "generous" type of yielding is called a "release" (p. 162).

GOAL OF THE MOVEMENT First of all, the working trot is the pace you use to ride a horse during the warm-up since it's natural for the horse, requiring little muscle effort. Secondly, during schooling sessions it provides an opportunity to ask for—or recreate—the horse's natural impulsion. This is especially true for horses worked a lot in collection. Asking repeatedly for the working trot in between collected work prevents the rider from merely riding more slowly, rather than properly shortening the horse's stride and shifting his weight back on his haunches. Frequently alternating between working and collected trot keeps the horse working from his haunches and back, thus developing his strength. This strength will benefit every other movement you ride, and will also become

A working trot at the beginning (left) and the end (right) of the warm-up phase. You can see how the trot became more expressive as the session went on.

important later on when you ride in collection for longer periods of time, and also when more extreme collection is necessary, such as during the piaffe (p. 95).

FAST FACTS Basic exercise; required at Training Level and First Level dressage tests (Preliminary and Novice in the UK), as well as in Young Horse Tests; loosens up the horse.

PYRAMID FACTOR Rhythm**, relaxation/suppleness***, contact***, impulsion***, straightness**, collection.

WORKING CANTER

A pace within the canter gait that encourages the horse's hind hooves to touch the ground slightly ahead of the front hooves—a length of stride between that of the collected and medium paces—as can be seen by the horse's hoofprints.

HOW IT'S SUPPOSED TO LOOK The working canter, taught to the young and uneducated horse before collection, must be ridden energetically forward with a slight uphill tendency and in a clear three-beat rhythm. The horse must be securely on the aids, "through" the poll, and as "straight" as possible.

MOST COMMON MISTAKES The Horse: exhibits a too "dull" tempo; does not have a clear three-beat rhythm; is downhill—on the forehand; is "nodding" in the poll; is tight in the neck; is not "through" the poll (i.e., his neck is stretched out straight forward); is above the bit; is on two tracks—not "straight."

CORRECT AIDS In the working canter, flex the horse at the poll slightly to the inside (as at all variations of the canter) while positioning your outside leg a hand's width behind the girth in a "guarding" position, and using the inside leg to "drive" at the girth. This encourages the horse's inside hind leg to "jump" more forward, which helps raise the horse's back and contribute to the desired "uphill" nature of the canter. In the canter, you must smoothly follow the horse's movement, "wiping" the saddle a bit with your seat in the canter rhythm. Imagine moving your hips forward and through your hands.

In order to maintain "freshness" in a working canter, it's helpful to ride transitions within the gait. Increasing the pace, then decreasing and increasing it again, encourages the horse to bend and lower his haunches, thus taking up more of his weight and developing thrust. The muscle strength this builds over time will also positively affect the "expression" of the working canter. Even horses that have become used to moving sluggishly as a result of incorrect riding can be "reactivated" this way.

GOAL OF THE MOVEMENT

You can always "recreate" a horse's engagement by returning to the working canter. Riding for too long in a collected gait can cause a rider to "pinch" with one or both legs, and result in a tight back in the horse. In addition, with a horse that is still developing, collected work can cause fatigue and subsequent sluggishness. Interspersing periods of a "fresh" working pace into your collected exercises prevents this from happening.

Riding transitions within the gait promotes animation in the working canter.

FAST FACTS Basic exercise; required at Training Level and First Level dressage tests (Preliminary and Novice in the UK), as well as in Young Horse Tests; loosens up the horse.

PYRAMID FACTOR Rhythm**, relaxation/suppleness***, contact***, impulsion***, straightness**, collection.

CHANGING REIN OUT OF THE CIRCLE

Changing direction from one 20-meter circle into another through "X."

Length of reins

When riding, you must always readjust the length of your reins for each new movement. It should be done as unobtrusively as possible. Rein length is correct when you—with light contact—are able to hold your hands freely in an upright position about a hand's width above the pommel, with slightly bent elbows and your upper arms not moving behind your body. The more collected the horse, the shorter your reins will be.

HOW IT'S SUPPOSED TO LOOK When you plan to change rein out of a circle, continue riding on the 20-meter circle (p. 179) with lateral bend until you reach "X." At "X," the point where the horse's body is exactly parallel to the short sides of the arena—change the flexion and bend and enter a second circle with new lateral bend. In order to change flexion and bend, you must straighten the horse for about one horse's length. The transition from one circle to the next should be smooth and ridden at the same tempo.

You can change direction out of the circle at all three basic gaits. The point where you change bend ("X"), is also where you change your diagonal when rising at the trot, or change your lead at the canter.

If the new circle is to be ridden with a counter-bend, the flexion and bend of the first circle are maintained.

MOST COMMON MISTAKES The Horse: goes against the hand when changing flexion and bend. **The Rider:** deviates from the circle line; does not pass through "X"; does not clearly change the horse's flexion and bend; cuts across the circle(s) diagonally.

CORRECT AIDS In order to change rein out of the circle correctly, it helps to first visualize the bending lines of the circles. When you are able to do this, there won't be a problem when moving from one circle into the next. Just before passing through "X," shorten the inside rein a bit while creating the new flexion and bend, making sure your aids are smooth and gentle. At the same moment, your outside leg, which has been positioned *behind* the girth, slides forward so it is positioned *at* the girth, becoming the new inside leg. Your old inside leg, formerly positioned at the girth, now slides a bit behind the girth.

As the horse moves from one circle into the next, your upper body should slightly follow the movement so that your shoulders are always parallel to the horse's ears. Immediately upon entering the new circle, focus on the next visual point in the bending line.

GOAL OF THE MOVEMENT Changing rein out of the circle can, first of all, be used to simply change directions. This, of course, isn't the only advantage. The movement also offers a great opportunity to gymnasticize the horse on a big, bending line and ride the horse more "into" your outside rein. By changing rein out of the circle (and perhaps changing again into the next one) you gymnasticize the horse evenly.

Since 20-meter circles are relatively generously sized school figures and don't require a lot of "carrying power," this movement is suitable for young horses. In dressage tests it gives the judge clues about the rider's coordination skills, as well as the horse's "straightness" on both sides.

FAST FACTS Basic exercise; loosens up the horse; teaches lateral mobility; furthers "stepping" into the outside rein.

PYRAMID FACTOR Rhythm*, relaxation/suppleness***, contact***, impulsion**, straightness**, collection.

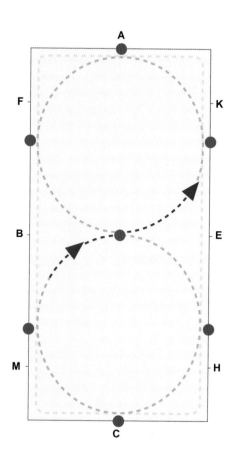

When changing rein out of the circle, the rider smoothly changes flexion and bend at "X."

HALF-VOLTE IN THE CORNER WITH RETURN TO THE TRACK

A teardrop-shaped arc of a circle ridden in a corner of the arena, with a diameter of 6, 8, or 10 meters, which creates a change of direction.

HOW IT'S SUPPOSED TO LOOK The half-volte in the corner with return to the track is ridden in the corner at the end of a long side of the arena. The first part consists of a half-circle, which you exit by riding straight back toward the long side of the arena in a change of direction. As in the regular volte (p. 171), the horse must first be flexed and bent evenly around the rider's inside leg, with the horse's poll the highest point and his ears level (indicating the head is not tipping to one side or the other). At the point where you precisely complete the first half of the volte, straighten the horse and ride back toward the track he came from, at an angle of approximately 45 degrees. The total size of the volte can vary—6, 8, or 10 meters— although in dressage tests it's specified.

MOST COMMON MISTAKES The Horse: is tight in the neck; has a tilted poll. **The Rider:** creates too big or too small a volte; pulls the horse around the turn; rides back toward the track in a travers-like manner.

CORRECT AIDS Begin the half-volte in the corner with return to the track as you would a simple turn: when you reach the corner, slightly bend the horse to the inside while giving a half-halt at the same time to prepare the horse for a new task. Your inside leg, placed at the girth, drives the horse's inside hind leg forward, while your outside leg lies slightly behind the girth, controlling the haunches and encouraging the horse to bend around your inside leg. After passing through the corner (which really is a quarter of your circle!) continue applying your aids to keep the horse turning and moving on into the *next* quarter.

Once the horse is bending correctly, softly yield your inside hand while keeping the outside rein taut enough to create a "boundary" for the horse's outside shoulder, but not so restrictive as to prevent the horse from stretching the muscles on the outside of his neck. This outer stretching is necessary or the horse will likely tilt his head at the poll. Maintain this flexion and bend until you have completed the half-volte, and you are looking toward the short side at the opposite end of the arena. At this point, instead of continuing a circle, give more with the inside rein while returning both legs to their original position at the girth, driving the horse evenly forward.

This way, the horse returns straight to the track in a diagonal line without any bend. In order not to run into the wall or fence, just before reaching the track, ride another slight turn until you are parallel to the wall or fence again. The whole movement is only complete when you're back on the track, in a straight line, facing the opposite direction.

The pattern of the half-volte in the corner with a return to the track goes back on a straight line.

It's easy to make mistakes in this movement, especially at the canter. When turning, the curve of the circle can be made too large, and when riding back toward the long side, there's the risk of riding a travers (p. 145). Both problems are caused—as is so often the case— by giving incorrect aids: when the half-volte is too big, the rider probably had too much inside rein and too little outside rein and leg. When the horse returns to the track in a travers position, this is usually caused by too much inside rein combined with a sideways-driving outside leg. In both cases, when training, it's helpful to ride the horse in counter-flexion for one or two strides in order to remember how he feels when turning.

GOAL OF THE MOVEMENT First of all, half-volte in the corner with return to the track is used to change direction, of course. It's also a great test to find out how the horse is ridden and if the rider is giving aids correctly. Furthermore, as with all turns and circles, its gymnasticizing effect is enormous. Because the horse has to take up more weight with his inside hind leg in the turn, his hindquarters are strengthened. Although after exiting the half-volte the movement is less strenuous, the remaining steps still require more coordination from both horse and rider. Therefore, it's quite a good indicator of whether a rider's foundation is correct (or incorrect).

FAST FACTS The level of difficulty depends on the size of the volte (the larger, the easier); can be ridden at all three basic gaits, up to a working pace (medium for a walk); develops strength and improves mobility.

PYRAMID FACTOR Rhythm**, relaxation/suppleness**, contact**, impulsion**, straightness**, collection*.

COUNTER-CANTER

A canter where the horse is flexed and bent toward the outside of the arena, circle, or turn, while on the opposite canter lead of the "true" canter—for example, cantering on the left lead when going to the right.

HOW IT'S SUPPOSED TO LOOK The foundation for the counter-canter movement is a balanced canter that allows for a minimum degree of collection. At the counter-canter the horse should—as in the "true" canter (p. 63) where the horse is on the "correct" lead for the direction of travel—exhibit a clear, three-beat rhythm and be flexed to the inside. Since the terms "inside" and "outside" are used in conjunction with a horse's flexion and bend and *not* with the horse and rider's position in the dressage arena, one still says a horse has "inside flexion" when in a counter-canter, even if it doesn't correspond with the inside of the arena. *The inside is always the direction toward which the horse is flexed or bent.*

When going around corners and other bending lines, such as circles, in the counter-canter, the horse must maintain the same flexion and bend and continue to "jump" under his body mass while exhibiting a balanced, clear, three-beat rhythm, with an uphill tendency, and with the hind legs tracking up.

MOST COMMON MISTAKES The Horse: exhibits an inconsistent tempo; shows little collection; loses rhythm (unclear three-beat rhythm; four-beat rhythm); switches leads; breaks into trot; throws his hindquarters to the outside in corners; travels in a "travers-like" manner; demonstrates little or incorrect flexion; is not quite balanced; is on the forehand; is tight in the neck; comes behind the vertical; goes against the rider's hand; exhibits a "seesawing" motion; nods his head too obviously; has a high croup.

CORRECT AIDS The counter-canter requires the same aids as the true canter—the only difference is that you are asking for the "wrong" lead for your direction of travel, and the horse is not flexed toward the inside of the arena or circle but toward the wall or outside of the circle. It's important to give a correct canter aid and have a good connection, especially on the curved lines, such as in corners. This helps the horse maintain his balance.

The less balanced a horse is, the more difficult the counter-canter will be, and the more likely he will switch leads or break into the trot. For this reason, when riding a young or inexperienced horse, give stronger aids in the beginning. This means: position the outside leg

The more balanced the regular canter, the better the counter-canter can be.

further behind the girth than you would normally, shift more weight onto your inside seat bone, and flex the horse to the inside more than usual. Also, riding "shallow" corners temporarily will make counter-canter easier. When a horse tends to evade with his haunches and lean on the outside rein (remember, "outside" means *outside the bend*), it most often helps to ride a few counter-canter strides in counter-flexion—that is, with the horse flexed to the inside of the arena or circle while still on the counter lead.

GOAL OF THE MOVEMENT The counter-canter is required at First Level (Novice in the UK) and above to test collection and balance. Furthermore, riding counter-canter improves collection since the horse must take up more weight with his haunches on bending lines (such as corners and circles) in order not to lose his balance. For this reason, including counter-canter in your work is more than just an exercise for the next dressage test; it also improves the horse's "carrying power"; balance; ability to "jump through" at the canter; loftiness of gait; and "straightness" (especially in the context of counter-flexion).

FAST FACTS Required at First Level (Novice in the UK) and above; develops collection and "carrying power."

PYRAMID FACTOR Rhythm*, relaxation/suppleness*, contact**, straightness**, collection***.

SITTING TROT
The rider remains seated in the saddle at the trot.

HOW IT'S SUPPOSED TO LOOK Like other elements of the rider's entire seat, the sitting trot should be balanced. This means that the rider should sit smoothly, absorbing the motion of the horse *without* disturbing him with endless body rocking or exaggerated hand, arm, and head movements. In the dressage seat, your upper body remains upright, and your legs lie with relaxed muscles against the horse's body at a slight angle. Your heels, hips, and shoulders create a vertical line. Your upper arms hang down in a relaxed manner, with your lower arms creating an angle so that there's a straight line from your hands to the reins to the horse's mouth. Depending on the degree of collection, the lower arm and upper arm create a greater or smaller angle. However, it should never be smaller than 90 degrees.

MOST COMMON MISTAKES The Rider: leans forward or leans back; has busy lower legs; pinches with her thighs; bounces instead of swinging with the motion; has a stiff midsection; collapses in the hip; hollows her back; pushes her lower legs too far forward (chair seat); pulls her lower legs too far backward; has a too loose or too tight seat.

CORRECT AIDS Since the sitting trot is not a movement but a type of seat, there are no aids to explain. However, you can train and improve the sitting trot. This requires seat correction from an instructor on a regular basis, as well as "internalizing" the correct way of sitting. Only practice will enable riders to automatically analyze themselves, and where and when necessary, make corrections. This requires many years of experience and a lot of feel.

Dr. Britta Schöffmann, seen riding her mare La Picolina at the sitting trot.

GOAL OF THE MOVEMENT The sitting trot—as a type of seat—quite simply is one of the basics of "being on a horse." But there's more to it than that: sitting the trot correctly makes work with the horse possible, as of course does a correct seat in general. But it is especially at the sitting trot that faults in a rider's seat may have serious consequences. A vicious cycle can be created: the rider whose sitting trot is incorrect or poor is not able to give aids effectively and "drive" the horse over the back, into the bit. This causes the horse's body to become disconnected, so he tightens his back muscles, making it more difficult for the rider to sit smoothly—which, as you can imagine, causes her seat to deteriorate even further. It's like chasing your own tail! Not only is a bouncing, "loud" sitting trot a rider fault that is marked down in a dressage test, it also makes it more than obvious to the judges that there are problems with the horse that might not have been so evident at first. A horse that's been worked correctly "allows" the rider to sit smoothly and comfortably.

FAST FACTS Type of seat at the trot; can be ridden in all paces.

PYRAMID FACTOR Rhythm**, relaxation/suppleness***, contact**, impulsion**, straightness*, collection**.

CHANGING REIN THROUGH THE CIRCLE

Changing direction by riding through the center of a 20-meter circle, from the open side of the circle toward the closed side of the circle.

HOW IT'S SUPPOSED TO LOOK Changing rein through the circle is ridden on an "S"-shaped line, from the point on the side of the circle "open" to the long side of the arena to the point on the side of the circle facing the short side of the arena (see diagram). The center of the "S-" shaped arc lies on the centerline. So, while on a 20-meter circle (p. 179), after passing the short side of the arena, turn at the next circle point and ride a 10-meter half circle toward the centerline (but looking toward the end of the arena), then change flexion and bend, and ride—again on a 10-meter half circle—toward the circle point on the opposite long side. From there continue on the 20-meter circle, now traveling in the opposite direction. During the entire exercise, the horse should remain securely on the aids and change flexion and bend smoothly.

MOST COMMON MISTAKES The Horse: exhibits little lateral bend; gets too tight; is on the forehand; goes against the rider's hand; changes flexion and bend awkwardly or roughly. **The Rider:** starts at the wrong circle point (the closed side of the circle); plans poorly (arcs are of uneven size); "S" curves too shallow or too steep.

CORRECT AIDS The rider who has mastered the aids for turning and for riding voltes (pp. 1 and 171) won't have any difficulty changing rein through the circle successfully. Just before reaching the first circle point, slightly increase the inside flexion so the horse leaves the track. At the same time, shift more weight onto the inside seat bone. Your inside leg remains at the girth and the outside leg slightly behind the girth. The inside leg activates the horse's inside hind leg, while the outside leg and a slightly forward "giving" hand keep the hindquarters and shoulders aligned. This way you ride a turn until reaching the centerline, where you change flexion and bend smoothly onto a second turn. (When riding this movement at the canter, change leads at this point, too.) The rein that has been the outside rein now becomes the inside rein, the leg that has been the outside leg slides forward toward the girth, and the formerly inside leg slides behind the girth. When changing flexion and bend, you should already focus on the circle point that's approaching. This ensures that the second arc of the "S" is the same size as the first one.

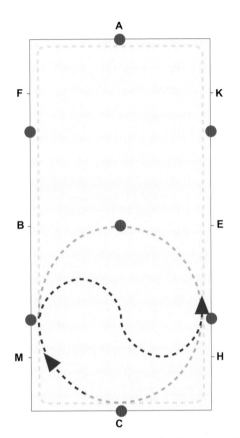

The change through the circle always begins on the side of the circle that opens onto the long side of the arena.

GOAL OF THE MOVEMENT First of all, changing rein through the circle is a simple way to change direction. It also tests the rider's influence on the horse. Furthermore, it's a more difficult form of the exercise changing rein out of the circle (p. 22) since it is ridden on smaller arcs, which increases the gymnasticizing effect on the horse.

FAST FACTS Basic exercise; suitable for the end of the warm-up as well as the work phase; can be ridden in all medium and collected paces at all three basic gaits; improves lateral mobility.

PYRAMID FACTOR Rhythm*, relaxation/suppleness**, contact**, impulsion*, straightness**, collection*.

CHANGING REIN ACROSS THE LONG DIAGONAL

The change of direction from left to right rein or vice versa via a diagonal line that always begins after the second corner of a short side, going toward the diagonally opposite corner of the arena.

HOW IT'S SUPPOSED TO LOOK Changing rein across the long diagonal consists of two individual parts: the turning part (p. 1) and riding straight ahead. When executed correctly, the horse goes deeply into the corner flexed and bent to the inside, then leaves the track exactly at the letter that is your turning point ("F," "M," "H," or "K"). Then the horse moves straight across the arena to complete the diagonal. At the next turning point, the horse again flexes and bends to the inside, and you ride deeply into the corner. If you ride this exercise at the rising trot, you change the diagonal at the second turning point. And, at the canter you also change leads at the second turning point.

MOST COMMON MISTAKES The Horse: crosses diagonal in a travers-like manner. **The Rider:** turns too early or too late; doesn't riding from letter to letter; strays from the diagonal line; arrives at the track too early or too late.

CORRECT AIDS Focus on the first turning point several feet before beginning the exercise. This helps you start on the diagonal line exactly at the letter. Apply the aids for turning, and move on to your next set of aids as soon as all four of the horse's legs are on the diagonal line. When the turn is done correctly, it's much easier to hit the diagonal line. During the turn, you should already be focused on the next turning point and ride straight toward it using forward driving aids. If, in the meantime, you look down or give a strong, one-sided leg aid, you'll easily deviate from the diagonal line, swerving off it. When this happens, say at the medium trot or canter (pp. 85 and 89), additional mistakes can occur, such as in the rhythm of the trot, or during lead changes at the canter. As soon as the horse's nose arrives at the turning point on the opposite long side, flex the horse once again to the inside, and bend him around your inside leg in order to be able to ride properly into the next corner.

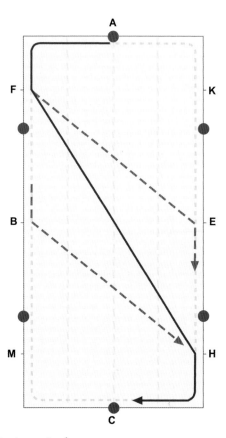

You can change reins when riding the long diagonal or the short diagonal.

GOAL OF THE MOVEMENT First of all, changing rein across the long diagonal is a school figure you can use to simply change direction. It's required at Training Level (Preliminary in the UK), where it gives judges an impression of the rider's influence on her horse. Furthermore, in more advanced dressage it's a movement on which others are based—movements that are ridden on this diagonal line away from the track include lengthenings (p. 153), flying changes of lead (p. 45), tempi changes (p. 131), and pirouettes (p. 99).

FAST FACTS Basic exercise; required from Training Level tests (Preliminary in the UK) to Grand Prix; can be ridden at all paces and basic gaits.

PYRAMID FACTOR Rhythm, relaxation/suppleness*, contact*, impulsion*, straightness*, collection.

Earning points in a dressage test

You can gain extra points by riding the arena figures accurately. On the other hand, you can lose points, too, when you don't ride from letter to letter, or figures in the correct shape.

CHANGING REIN ACROSS THE SHORT DIAGONAL

The change of direction from left to right rein or vice versa via a diagonal line that always begins after the second corner of a short side, leading toward the middle of the opposing long side of the arena.

HOW IT'S SUPPOSED TO LOOK This school figure is basically ridden in the same way as changing rein across the long diagonal (p. 32). The only difference is the point of arrival, in this case, the *middle* of the long side at letters "E" or "B." Theoretically, instead of starting the diagonal after the corner of the short side, you could also turn at "E" or "B," and ride into the diagonal corner, as this also would be changing rein across the short diagonal. This version is only required at Training and First Level dressage tests (Preliminary and Novice in the UK).

MOST COMMON MISTAKES The Horse: crosses short diagonal in a travers-like manner. **The Rider:** turns too early or too late; doesn't ride from letter to letter; strays from the short diagonal line; arrives at the track too early or too late.

CORRECT AIDS See changing rein across the long diagonal, p. 32.

GOAL OF THE MOVEMENT Just as with changing across the long diagonal, this movement is primarily used to change direction. In addition, it's often used to introduce the counter-canter since the short diagonal doesn't end in a corner but leads onto the straight line of the long side—which, because it facilitates the act of balancing, makes it easier for horses at the beginning of their education, or horses not yet secure in their collection.

FAST FACTS Basic exercise; required at Training (Preliminary in the UK) to Grand Prix levels; can be ridden at all paces in all three basic gaits.

PYRAMID FACTOR Rhythm, relaxation/suppleness *, contact*, impulsion*, straightness*, collection.

RIDING DOWN THE CENTERLINE

Traveling on a straight line down the middle of the arena (from short end to short end) without changing direction.

HOW IT'S SUPPOSED TO

LOOK When executed correctly, the rider turns just before reaching the middle of the short side of the arena, enters the centerline via a quarter-volte, and rides straight down the centerline toward the middle of the opposite short side. Upon arrival there, you turn back onto the track through a quarter-volte *without* changing direction. Thus, if you begin the exercise tracking right, you also complete it tracking right, and vice versa. During the turn, the horse must be flexed to the inside and bent around your inside leg. When riding down the centerline, however, the horse must be perfectly straight.

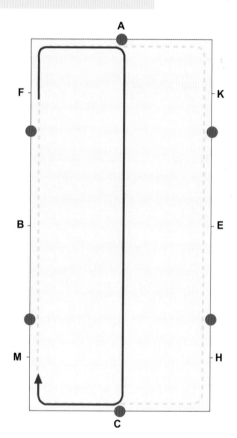

MOST COMMON MISTAKES

The Horse: evades through the outside shoulder during the turn; "wanders"; sways; is on two tracks coming down the centerline. **The Rider:** turns too early or too late; doesn't ride exactly on the centerline; overshoots the centerline.

When riding down the centerline, you do not change direction but stay on the same rein.

CORRECT AIDS Especially when riding down the centerline, it's highly important to ride an accurate turn (p. 1). This is because when the turn is ridden incorrectly, you will not be able to hit the centerline at the

Riding down the centerline
requires a high degree of
concentration—and a
straight horse.

right spot. In order to turn onto the centerline you must, depending on the level of your horse's training, initiate the turn before the middle of the short side while focusing on the letters "A" or "C" (depending on which end you start). Note: the letters should set the *outer* boundary for the turn, so give yourself ample space to begin your turn *before* arriving at the letter.

Shortly after initiating the first turn, look toward the middle of the opposite short side until you turn again at the end of the centerline. Focusing on the letter will help you remain in better balance, making it easier to keep the horse straight.

In order to avoid the horse evading the turn through his outside shoulder, make an effort not to overuse the inside rein and instead yield with this hand at the right moment. The outside rein and outside leg should keep the horse's shoulder and haunches under control. If the horse still tends to evade to the outside despite these aids—perhaps because of his natural crookedness—it most often is helpful to briefly counterflex him (for one or two strides).

GOAL OF THE MOVEMENT Riding down the centerline is a school figure that tests the rider's influence on his horse as well as the horse's level of training. Mistakes that occur repeatedly, such as evasion through the outside shoulder when turning or "wandering" on the centerline, are signs of incorrect aids and a lack of "straightness." If, on the other hand, the exercise can be ridden without difficulty, it shows that the rider uses her aids correctly and the horse exhibits a certain degree of "throughness" to the aids.

FAST FACTS Basic exercise; can be ridden at all paces and basic gaits.

PYRAMID FACTOR Rhythm, relaxation/suppleness*, contact*, impulsion, straightness*, collection.

Riding down the
centerline.

CHANGING REIN DOWN THE CENTERLINE

Riding down the centerline and changing direction on the opposite short side of the arena.

HOW IT'S SUPPOSED TO LOOK

This movement should be ridden like riding down the centerline (p. 35)—at least until just before it's completed. The difference is that the rider changes direction at the end. This means that if you started out tracking left, you finish the exercise by tracking right and vice versa.

MOST COMMON MISTAKES The Horse:

evades through the outside shoulder; leaves the centerline; "wanders"; is on two tracks down the centerline. **The Rider:** turns too early or too late; is not exactly on the centerline; overshoots the centerline; forgets to change direction.

CORRECT AIDS See riding down the centerline, p. 35.

GOAL OF THE MOVEMENT See riding down the centerline, p. 35.

FAST FACTS Basic exercise; can be ridden at both medium and collected paces, with extensions possible on centerline.

When changing the rein down the centerline, you change direction when you reach the end of the center-line.

PYRAMID FACTOR Rhythm, relaxation/suppleness*, contact*, impulsion, straightness*, collection.

Cantering off on
the left lead.

SIMPLE CHANGE OF LEAD

Changing from a left-lead canter to a right-lead canter— or vice versa—through the walk.

HOW IT'S SUPPOSED TO LOOK A simple change goes well when the horse, from a clear, three-beat canter, promptly and smoothly transitions into the walk without hesitation and while remaining securely on the aids. Then, when given the canter aid after three or four walk steps, the horse spontaneously picks up the other lead.

MOST COMMON MISTAKES The Horse: "dribbles" into the walk; changes via the trot ("jigs" before resuming canter); doesn't exhibit a clear transition to walk prior to resuming canter; is tense; uses too few or too many walk steps; is on the forehand; is tight in the neck; is against the hand; doesn't exhibit a spontaneous canter depart. **The Rider:** requests change too early or too late;

CORRECT AIDS Two basic requirements allow the rider to execute the simple change successfully: 1) the horse is securely on the aids; and 2) the quality of the canter is good. Only when both conditions are in place will the change work correctly in all its individual parts.

First of all, you must focus on the point where the change is to be performed. If, for example, you are asked to "do a simple canter change in the middle of the short side of the arena," you must begin by transitioning to the walk just before reaching "A" or "C," continuing with three to four walk steps until just passing "A" or "C," then promptly cantering off again on the new lead. To initiate the simple change, give a half-halt to prepare your horse for the new task ahead, then follow up with additional half-halts. At the same time, slide your outside leg, which has been placed behind the girth at the canter, forward into its original position. For a brief moment, the restraining aids prevail while simultaneously driving the horse evenly forward with both legs. When done correctly, the horse compresses his body a bit, takes up more weight on his hind legs and transitions from the canter right into the walk. At that moment, you must react quickly and "let" him walk by moving both your hands very slightly forward, followed by a gentle, forward-driving aid from both legs. This allows the horse to stretch into your hand and find his rhythm at the walk.

During this brief walk phase, silently and calmly count the number of steps, and on the third or fourth *at the latest*, give the aid for resuming the canter (p. 5). Again, give a half-halt on the outside rein, slightly flex the horse in the poll to the inside with the inside rein, while at the same time positioning your outside leg behind the girth, while the inside leg is at the girth providing a brief, go-forward aid. At the moment the horse is about to pick up the canter, soften the inside rein slightly, allowing "room" for the canter stride to happen.

GOAL OF THE MOVEMENT First of all, a simple canter change is used to move from one canter lead to the other without having to perform a flying change of lead (p. 45). It is also—when ridden correctly—an incredibly useful and good exercise to gymnasticize the horse—it improves "throughness," especially when you frequently ride several simple changes in a row. The orchestration of the various

aids, the alternating between "gathering" the horse together and riding on (which you need for the downward transition to the walk as well as the canter depart), sends the horse more toward your hand from back to front and causes him to flex his hind joints and lower his hindquarters a bit more. At the same time, the frequent changing from the left to the right lead, or vice versa, alternately stretches and contracts the muscles on both sides of his body, which improves the horse's "straightness." For these reasons, you cannot ride simple canter changes too often. They are ideal at the end of warm-up and during the work phase to either prepare the horse for collection or improve it, as well as to build muscles in the hindquarters and encourage the "letting through" of the aids.

FAST FACTS Progressive exercise; suitable for both the end of warm-up and the work phase; can be ridden in a working and collected canter; improves coordination and "carrying power."

PYRAMID FACTOR Rhythm**, relaxation/suppleness**, contact***, impulsion**, straightness***, collection***.

The simple canter change via the walk proceeds from one canter lead to another: as shown here, a left lead into a right lead canter.

The moment of suspension when the horse changes his canter lead.

FLYING CHANGE OF LEAD

Changing from left lead canter to right lead canter—and vice versa—at the moment of the highest point of the canter suspension phase, without transitioning downward to the walk or trot.

HOW IT'S SUPPOSED TO LOOK Flying changes of lead are an advanced exercise. When executed correctly, the horse changes from one canter lead to the other at the rider's request during the "highest" point of the canter suspension phase when all four feet are off the ground. The new "leading" front and hind leg should change simultaneously (when the front lead changes while the hind does not, the horse is said to be "cross-cantering"; and when one leg changes before the other, the horse is said to be "late"—see below).

The prerequisite for a good flying change is a correct, balanced, and "big" canter stride. When this is the case, the moment of suspension gives the horse enough time to switch leading legs cleanly. The better quality the horse's canter, the more beautiful the flying changes can be.

MOST COMMON MISTAKES The Horse: is late (new front "leading" leg changes before the hind); changes his hind leg first (new hind leading leg changes before the front); lacks impulsion; responds slowly to the rider's aids (horse changes one canter stride or more after the rider gives the aid); has a high croup; has a tight neck; does a "flat" or "shallow" change; "sways" through the changes; is crooked; goes against the rider's hand; is rushed or tense; breaks from canter.

CORRECT AIDS To give a correct aid for the flying change on a trained horse is one thing; to train flying changes to a green horse another. The latter requires a lot of experience and therefore should only be done by advanced riders. After all, the flying change under saddle presents quite a demanding sequence of motion for the horse. When at liberty and without a rider, young horses often manage to perform flying changes naturally, since they are generally in a state of balance. The addition of a rider disturbs this balance so it must be recreated through systematic training—and when a rider makes mistakes during this process, they are destined to become problematic later when training flying changes. Once mistakes have been learned, such as changing late or not "jumping through," they are very difficult to eliminate since they are quickly "automated" in the horse's movement pattern.

When riding a flying change on a horse that has been trained to do them, it is best to begin by changing from the counter-canter to the correct-lead canter, as this is easier for most horses. To develop a feel for the changes, it is helpful to change across the short diagonal (p. 34). Doing so changes your direction and allows you to vary the angle at which you approach the opposite track (as opposed to changing across the long diagonal—p. 32—where you end up in the corner of the arena).

On the counter lead, travel across the short diagonal and approach the point where you will ask for the flying change just before reaching the track. Apply pressure with your outside leg behind the

Flying changes require the horse to have a solid canter, and the rider, excellent coordination.

girth to "wake up" the horse's inside hind leg and encourage him to "jump" forward when given the aid for the change (note: you are not driving him *sideways*, you are driving him *forward*). Give a half-halt to prepare the horse and when you are ready, apply the following finely coordinated aids at the same time: slightly flex the horse toward the new leading canter leg and switch the position of your own legs (the old inside leg that was at the girth should now be behind the girth, and vice versa). At the moment of the flying change, give with your new inside hand, allowing the horse's new leading hind leg to "jump" through and the canter stride to appear "uphill."

During the flying change your hip and weight shift slightly toward the new "inside." However, do not exaggerate this weight shift as it can unbalance the horse, deteriorating or even preventing the change. The best—and most correct way—to ride the flying change is with only the slightest use of your body. This is possible, however, only when on a trained horse. A green or young horse often requires the rider to give much more explicit aids in order to help him understand what you want, and exerting a stronger influence with your upper body can sometimes be quite useful—in essence, deliberately unbalancing the horse, and thereby causing him to switch leads.

GOAL OF THE MOVEMENT The flying change is, just like the simple change (p. 41), an opportunity to change direction without having to ride too many rounds at the counter-canter. However, it allows you to do so without transitioning to another gait first. Flying changes are also a good way of testing a horse's relaxation and suppleness, and his "straightness"—the second and fifth elements in the Training Pyramid. Only a horse that is relaxed and correctly aligned is able to perform clean and beautiful flying changes. Tension that's latent or new often erupts at the moment of changing and signals an absence of relaxation, just as a lack in "straightness" will prevent an even flying change.

Taking breaks

Take a break! This applies to riding, also. Just like us, horses get tired. Strenuous work tires their muscles (creating lactic acid) and disrupts concentration. For this reason, repeating the same movement over and over is useless. In the long run, the movement will just get worse and worse, and in the worst cases, produce resistance. Instead, after 15 minutes of work—at the most—take a break and rest at the walk. And, by performing a variety of exercises rather than the same one, you'll relax the horse, which helps to further his training.

Note: a single well-executed flying change is the prerequisite for tempi changes (p. 131), which are required in upper level dressage tests.

FAST FACTS Advanced exercise; suitable for both the end of warm-up and the work phase; can be ridden in a collected, working, and medium canter; improves coordination.

Many riders ask themselves the following question: "Should I work first on counter-canter (left) or flying changes (right)?"

PYRAMID FACTOR Rhythm, relaxation/suppleness, contact, impulsion, straightness, collection.

Counter-canter or flying changes, first?

"Should a horse be able to perform a solid counter-canter before attempting flying changes? This is a question many riders ask in the course of training. I believe a rider should accept everything a horse offers of his own accord. When a young horse changes his leads on his own, accept it gratefully, and reward him. This is because every horse learns counter-canter, but not necessarily the flying changes. For this reason, you should not adamantly practice the counter-canter first or even punish the horse if he switches leads but praise him instead. The more a horse comes into balance, the easier the counter-canter is anyway. Flying changes, on the other hand, are more likely to cause problems. Therefore a rider should view a changing of the lead as a gift and accept it gratefully."

DR. UWE SCHULTEN-BAUMER SEN.
Olympic trainer, dressage patron

FULL HALT

The concurrence of all aids resulting in the horse coming to a complete, square, straight stop.

HOW IT'S SUPPOSED TO LOOK A full halt is successful when the horse transitions smoothly yet promptly into the halt from the walk, trot, or canter; remains quietly and securely on the rider's aids; and distributes his weight evenly on all four legs.

MOST COMMON MISTAKES The Horse: "dribbles" into the halt (via the walk or trot); is on the forehand; goes against the rider's hand; is tight in the neck; is crooked; evades through his haunches; stops too abruptly. **The Rider:** uses too much hand; falls forward or backward.

CORRECT AIDS According to the definition of the movement, at the full halt all the rider's aids must be simultaneous. When you plan to transition to the halt—that is, to *apply* a *full halt*—you must drive the horse forward while maintaining rein pressure and giving a weight aid.

Let's begin with the restraining rein aid, which acts like a car's brake, so to speak. However, on a horse, you "brake" only briefly and always in combination with using the "accelerator"—your driving leg aids. Why? The reason is simple: pressure causes counter-pressure; traction causes counter-traction. If you pull on the reins alone, the horse will just get long in his back and pull against you with his neck and body, as if he were pulling a carriage. The rider keeps pulling, as does the horse—and the full halt has failed. In contrast, when the rein aid is combined with a forward-driving leg aid, the horse's hind legs are animated to step more forward and carry more weight. The process prevents the horse from becoming "longer," and in fact, the horse appears to compress himself or "close up," and his forehand is unburdened as he comes to a halt.

Halt and salute.

Controlled use of the seat and weight aids during the full halt is also important. After all, the horse is supposed to compress in order to be

The full halt consists of "gathering" the horse together, driving him "through," and halting.

able to halt correctly. In order to do this, he must be encouraged to raise his back. This is only possible, however, when you cease the forward-driving aids and remain still, sitting vertically on the horse in perfect balance. Many riders tend to lean backward during the full halt, perhaps even throwing their legs forward as if stepping on the brakes in their car. A horse, obviously, is *not* a car, and on top of that, is very sensitive, especially in his back! By leaning backward, a rider puts an enormous amount of pressure on the horse's back muscles, which the horse will try to escape by moving forward. And when the rider pushes his legs forward as well, the horse's hind legs trail out behind him, his back hollows, and the pressure he feels on his back is intensified. If anything, when riding a horse that tends to lean against the hand, you should slightly and briefly lean *forward*. It is ideal, of course, to sit vertically and completely balanced, and execute the full halt with the slightest of aids.

Repeat the correct restraining and driving aids until the horse has halted. With a horse that allows the aids to come "through," this can happen after your first combined application of aids. But, with horses that are less "through" or not yet well trained, you can expect a delay in their response, which can only be eliminated in the course of further training.

GOAL OF THE MOVEMENT Full halts, like almost all movements, serve a variety of purposes. First of all, they are an absolute necessity for controlling a horse, and consequently are the equivalent of skiing's "snow plow," or even its emergency brake—sitting down! Only the rider who is able to stop—whether on the ski slope or in the saddle— is able to prevent potentially dangerous situations and accidents.

In a dressage test, full halts test the horse's "throughness" to the aids, and give judges an idea of how the horse has been worked and whether the rider is influencing the horse correctly. In addition, full halts are a wonderful tool to use in the training of a horse. Integrating as many of them as possible in work at the walk, trot, and later, the canter, together with the combination of the various aids and physical actions requested of the horse (lowering the haunches, raising the back, and stretching toward the bit) provides an excellent gymnasticzing effect—provided, of course, they are executed correctly. The more correct the full halt is executed, the suppler the entire horse will become.

FAST FACTS Basic exercise; suitable for both the end of the warm-up and the work phase; can be ridden from all basic gaits; improves "carrying power."

PYRAMID FACTOR Rhythm*, relaxation/suppleness**, contact***, impulsion***, straightness**, collection***.

> ### "Breathing" hands
>
> A "quiet" hand must not be confused with a "firm" hand. And, "yielding" the hands should not be "throwing the reins away." Imagine your hands are "breathing." Visualize this to keep just enough flexibility.

SALUTE
Performing a halt and facing the judges in order to physically greet them at the beginning and the end of a dressage test.

HOW IT'S SUPPOSED TO LOOK Saluting is one of the very first requirements in a dressage test and for this reason, should not be underestimated. The rider leaves a positive or negative impression on the judges at both the beginning and the end of a test, depending on the quality of the salute. This movement isn't commonly viewed as a rider's signature for nothing!

In general, the salute is made on the centerline (except when riding in a group) and most commonly at "X"—though it is sometimes also at "G," in front of the judges. To salute, take both reins in one hand and greet the judges with your free hand. Female riders simply let their free hand drop to the side of their body (in lower level classes, it is usually the hand that carries the whip) while crisply nodding their head once at the same moment. Male riders lift their helmet, bowler, or top hat, drop the hand with the hat

During the salute, the horse must stand quietly, and on all four legs evenly.

briefly, and then replace the hat. During this, it's important for the horse to stand straight and parallel to the long side; remain immobile; distribute his weight evenly on all four feet; and stay on the bit with his poll the highest point. After saluting, take up the reins to proceed.

MOST COMMON MISTAKES The Horse: doesn't halt precisely at the required letter; stands crookedly; halts not square; steps backward; comes behind the vertical; throws his head; fidgets. **The Rider:** loses contact; loses a rein during the salute or when taking up reins again.

CORRECT AIDS The salute contains all sorts of pitfalls, which can be avoided with practice—and it can be practiced in all its individual parts. This includes the salute itself, since many horses tend to get fidgety at exactly the moment when the rider takes both reins in one hand, or lifts his hat. And, some horses want to immediately walk off after the salute without waiting for the rider's aid.

Riders practicing their salute.

To begin, turn onto the centerline (p. 35) and at the required letter, ride a correct full halt (p. 49). As soon as the horse halts, quietly salute—even if there are no judges because you're at home schooling. Instead, simply greet the wall, the mirror, or a few amused spectators. Only by repeatedly practicing this way will the horse learn to stand quietly while you take both reins into one hand, salute, then take up the reins again, and finally, give the aid for the walk.

When rehearsing, take a great deal of care to train the horse to remain standing quietly until you give him the aid to walk on. In a dressage test it's different: although it certainly is required that you remain still, an experienced rider will "accept it" if his horse walks off of his own accord at the end of the salute, or at the moment he's gathered the reins again. This is because if, in such a situation, the rider prevents his horse from moving forward, the halt itself could be disrupted and marked down, resulting in a lower score. Walking on a bit too early, on the other hand, rarely attracts attention.

GOAL OF THE MOVEMENT The salute is one of the few exercises that, apart from testing the horse's obedience, has no value in training or gymnasticizing the horse. It has its roots in equestrian tradition and expresses courteous behavior between judge and rider at the beginning and the end of a dressage test.

FAST FACTS Basic exercise.

PYRAMID FACTOR Rhythm, relaxation/suppleness, contact, impulsion, straightness, collection.

Movements are means to an end

"The bottom line of dressage training is to improve the underlying, basic qualities of a horse, and do so harmoniously. Riding dressage movements should have nothing to do with just rattling off exercises, but with helping the horse in a systematic fashion to move under a rider more easily and with beauty—regardless of the level of training. The rider must free himself from thinking that he needs to practice movements for their own sake; they are not ends in themselves but means to an end. When your basic work is correct, the movements will fall in your lap–like a ripe apple. Practicing these movements without following the structure of the Training Pyramid, on the other hand, is counterproductive and incorrect. The rider might be lucky when the movements he has practiced this way turn out to be successful. But, when a horse performs like a robot, movements will lack expression and charm, have no gymnastic value whatsoever and he will not have matured physically or mentally.

"The movements must always be regarded as the means on the way to your ultimate goal, as stated above. The fact that in the end they can be seen to work so easily and smoothly is just icing on the cake."

CHRISTOPH HESS
Director of the department of training at the German Equestrian Federation, international dressage judge.

HALF-SCHOOL
Traveling the track of only one-half the size of the arena.

HOW IT'S SUPPOSED TO LOOK Being instructed to ride "half-school" is quite rare these days. And, although in modern dressage tests it isn't required at all, I would like to talk about this movement briefly. Dressage tests are frequently revised, and it could well happen that riding half-school will again become a requirement one day.

When you ride half-school, you must use the center point of one long side of the arena as a turning point, and from there proceed straight toward the center point on the opposite long side, then turn onto the track again without changing direction. Thereby you must take care not to overshoot the points "B" or "E" respectively. You must turn in time so that, after riding a quarter-volte, you precisely hit the line from "E" to "B" or vice versa.

MOST COMMON MISTAKES Similar to going "full school," going "half-school" is not particularly difficult. The only mistakes you might make are turning incorrectly—too early or too late—or riding a shallow corner.

CORRECT AIDS If you want to execute the half-school correctly, it's helpful to visualize the letters "B" and "E" respectively as the end of a square and the connection between these two letters as the arena track. When this is achieved, you shouldn't have any difficulties riding precise turns and hitting the track straight. Being able to turn correctly (p. 1) is a prerequisite for success.

GOAL OF THE MOVEMENT Riding half school tests the rider's influence on the horse and how well the horse is trained.

FAST FACTS Basic exercise; can be ridden in all three gaits in collected and working paces.

The interplay of hand, seat, and leg.

PYRAMID FACTOR Rhythm, relaxation/suppleness*, contact*, impulsion, straightness*, collection.

HALF-HALT

The "tool" the rider uses to prepare the horse for each new movement and transition.

HOW IT'S SUPPOSED TO LOOK A half-halt is not a movement; it is not even an exercise. Rather it is a combination of aids you use to get the horse's attention and "gather" and rebalance him more between your seat, leg, and rein. Half-halts are applied whenever you want something from your horse—whether a new movement or a transition from one gait into the next, or from one pace into another. Thereby, the horse should always maintain his rhythm, stay relaxed, and remain on the bit.

MOST COMMON MISTAKES The Horse: goes against the rider's hand; lacks "throughness" to the aids; doesn't step under with the hind legs; tenses his back. **The Rider:** uses too obvious or too strong aids.

In this photo, the horse should be bringing his haunches more underneath his center of gravity during the half-halt.

CORRECT AIDS As I said before, the half-halt is in essence an aid in itself, and one of the most important ones, too. Nonetheless, many riders have a rather vague idea of what they are supposed to do up there on the horse! A half-halt requires feel and intuition, and it turns out best when it is executed automatically—without thinking too much about it.

The half-halt is a combination of an increased seat aid (bracing the small of the back), leg aids (brief pressure on both sides), and restraining rein aids (fists remain in same position, but are slightly turned inward), and is *always* followed by a brief yielding of the hands. This means you drive the horse forward while holding him back at the same time. You "compress" the horse a bit like a coiled spring under tension. When the horse accepts this by swinging more under his body with his hind legs, you can feel it. The horse "sits"—he "comes back to you." Depending on the movement you are preparing for, your next aids will need to be intensified somewhat, either forward, sideways, or restraining.

The rider who has problems "feeling" the correct half-halt, should try to think of what it is like to halt (p. 49) during the half-halt. At the exact moment the horse wants to "accept" the aids to halt, you must instead drive him forward again. If you can achieve this smoothly a few times in a row without the horse actually coming to a halt, you— and your horse—are beginning to understand the half-halt.

GOAL OF THE MOVEMENT If the aids can be called "letters of communication" between horse and rider, with the movements the "sentences," then half-halts are the "words." Only when the words are placed correctly will the sentences work. When executing a correct half-halt, the horse should step more into the rider's hand, contact and relaxation should improve, and—subsequently—impulsion and collection.

FAST FACTS Important foundation tool; used constantly and is essential for all good riding; produces coordination and "carrying power."

PYRAMID FACTOR Rhythm***, relaxation/suppleness***, contact***, impulsion***, straightness***, collection***.

The key to riding

"Executing half-halts correctly is one of the most difficult tasks. First, you must learn to ask the horse to do a few more engaged steps and strides before each corner by coordinating your seat and leg aids. Pulling on the reins doesn't get the rider anywhere–on the contrary. Inexperienced riders are best taught how to perform a half-halt on a trained horse that already knows it well. I have every rider transition to the walk before the corner and have him trot or canter again immediately. This is supposed to help him understand how it feels when a horse swings his hind legs underneath his body, takes up more weight onto his hindquarters, and rounds the back. Only then do I allow a rider to ride half-halts within a gait. Half-halts must be like second nature, and for me, only then does riding begin."

MARTIN SCHAUDT
Team Olympic medalist,
Team European Championship
medalist

HALTING
Coming to a standstill in hand or under the rider.

HOW IT'S SUPPOSED TO LOOK The rider must be able to halt her horse at any letter in the dressage ring—with, or sometimes without, the support of the arena fence or wall. Halting always develops from a full halt (p. 49). At the halt, the horse should be standing square and be "through" in the poll while distributing his weight on all four legs as evenly as possible. He must stand and wait quietly for the rider's next aids to come. Although the movement sounds easy, there are many opportunities for mistakes since halting requires relaxation, correct contact, and good balance.

MOST COMMON MISTAKES The Horse: fidgets; halts not square (a leg is forward or backward); displays an "open" halt (one or both hind legs trail far out behind); rests (cocks one hind leg or the other); is wide behind; steps back; is tight in the neck; is behind the vertical; is above the bit; evades contact; throws his head; doesn't come to an immediate, immobile halt.

This halt is not square.

This halt is square and straight.

CORRECT AIDS Even though halting might appear to be quite a passive exercise, the rider is actually not totally inactive when standing still. As mentioned earlier, you come to a halt by applying the aids for a full halt. When these are given correctly, the horse will transition to a good halt—most of the time.

Once your horse has come to a halt you mustn't simply "take a break"—if you do, the horse will probably forget about the aids you just used, have a look at his surroundings, and maybe just keep walking! You need to keep the aids *on*, though much less intensively, cutting them back to a minimum, so to speak. Sit vertically in the center of the saddle, with your lower legs lying at the girth, or slightly behind the girth, and allow them to "breathe" along with your hands. This means you apply the tiniest half-halts to maintain the horse's posture. The more secure and balanced a horse is on the aids at the halt, the less you have to do. If, however, your horse tends to push against your hands, evading the contact, you'll need to apply more forward-driving pressure with your legs in combination with an upright torso and gently restraining hands. As soon as the horse yields in the poll and chews on the bit, you can soften your hands and allow your legs to lie passively again.

Halting correctly can be a challenge for a young horse that hasn't yet found his balance underneath the rider—even when standing still. To compensate for this lack of balance, he will tend to stand with his legs more "open"—picture a sailor standing with his legs wide apart on a ship to counteract the rocking of the waves. The better the horse has already found his "sea legs," the easier it'll be for him to halt correctly.

The horse's own imbalance or lack of "straightness," or crookedness in the rider, can also cause the horse to halt with his legs too "open." When this happens, your main goal must be to achieve correct balance and straightness while influencing the horse equally on both sides. The "emergency aid" to give when the horse has halted in an open stance is to ask him with your leg, or with a light touch of the whip, to bring the trailing hind leg squarely underneath his body. Note that an "open" halt must always be corrected forward, *never* backward, because that would teach the horse that it is acceptable to back up when halting.

In the past, some dressage tests explicitly demanded "five seconds of immobility." Today it is important to remember that such a time-frame is still part of the criteria for a correct halt, even if the exact amount of time required is not specified anymore.

GOAL OF THE MOVEMENT Although halting is required in dressage tests, it has many uses and is a prerequisite for safe, correct riding. Only the rider who is able to keep his horse still at the halt can wait until it is safe to proceed at a red traffic light or a railway crossing, for example. Consequently, for horses—animals of flight—halting is one of the most important exercises in obedience.

Furthermore, halting as a result of applying the aids for the full halt is an excellent test of whether the horse is truly letting the aids "through"—the better he does this, the better the quality of the halt. And, last but not least, halting is used as preparation for other move-ments, such as the salute (p. 51), the turn on the forehand (p. 174), the turn on the haunches (p. 65), and the rein-back (p. 114).

FAST FACTS Basic movement.

PYRAMID FACTOR Rhythm, relaxation/suppleness, contact, impul-sion, straightness, collection.

HALF-STEPS
Shortened trot steps with a reduced phase of suspension to prepare the horse for the piaffe.

HOW IT'S SUPPOSED TO LOOK Half-steps should only be ridden by experienced riders or under supervision. First of all, they are taught in preparation for the piaffe (p. 95), a very difficult movement, which is only suitable for advanced horses, and second, many riders can't feel the difference between proper half-steps and the horse just "slouching" along. When performing half-steps, the horse should show clearly shortened and rhythmically pure trot steps, collected with a shortened frame, and with increased flexion in the joints of the hindquarters as the hind legs continue to actively step under the center of the body's mass. The phase of suspension in the trot is definitively reduced. Furthermore, half-steps should always demonstrate a "forward" and "uphill" tendency.

When ridden correctly, half-steps develop the horse's ability to round his back, as well as increase his strength.

MOST COMMON MISTAKES The Horse: loses rhythm; trots too slowly; has too little activity behind; is on the forehand; "hovers"; drags his hind legs; trails his hind legs out behind; has a high croup; hollows his back; is tight in the neck; goes behind the vertical.

CORRECT AIDS The prerequisite for starting half-steps is a horse capable of a higher degree of collection and one that "lets the aids through." When this is the case, you can try to reduce the forward-ness and length of his trot strides by increasing your rein aids while simultaneously driving more with your back and legs. You must not sit too heavily and—to make it easier for the horse to raise his back—it may be best to take on a slightly *forward* seat. Position both legs slightly behind the girth to drive the horse's hind legs forward while you alternately restrain and yield with the reins.

Half-steps can also be developed from the collected walk; however, you must take care not to build up tension, which can lead to problems with the rhythm (pacing or jigging). You can also practice by further collecting the horse when riding at the collected trot, just as if you intend to ride a transition but change your mind at the last moment. And, for some horses it's easier to briefly transition from the trot down into the walk, then riding on immediately in half-steps.

At first, be content with a few half-steps in order to prevent rhythm faults from occurring and the horse becoming insecure.

GOAL OF THE MOVEMENT Half-steps are good preparation for the piaffe later on since they teach the horse to move in a trot-like manner with rhythmically pure and forward-swinging hind legs, and with a forward-and-upward tendency. Even if some horses will never be perfect at the piaffe because of unsuitable conformation or a lack of athletic ability, half-steps and the resulting increase in flexion in the haunches and hind-end weight-bearing will improve the trot overall.

FAST FACTS Advanced exercise; only for Third Level (Medium/

Advanced Medium in the UK) horses and above; produces "carrying power."

PYRAMID FACTOR Rhythm, relaxation/suppleness**, contact*, impulsion***, straightness, collection***.

"TRUE" CANTER

The three-beat gait where the horse is on the correct lead (the front and hind leg on the inside of the turn or the arena reach further forward than the front and hind leg on the outside), is flexed, and is bent toward the inside of the turn or arena.

HOW IT'S SUPPOSED TO LOOK The "true" canter with the inside legs leading (as opposed to the counter-canter—see p. 26) is the "normal," correct canter. The horse's body should be aligned, meaning that his hind feet should track straight into—or beyond—the prints of the front feet (*not* beside them). The canter's crucial attribute of execution is its clear, three-beat rhythm. The canter stride should be full of impulsion and "uphill," covering as much ground as possible.

MOST COMMON MISTAKES The Horse: four-beats (canter slows to the point where all four feet touch the ground separately); is crooked; is on two tracks; is on the forehand; doesn't cover ground; is croup-high; goes against the rider's hand; is tight in the neck; displays inconsistent contact. **The Rider:** asks for too much inside flexion.

CORRECT AIDS Whether riding in true canter or counter-canter, you must always sit straight in the center of the horse while putting slightly more weight onto your inside seat bone. Remember, the word "inside" doesn't necessarily refer to the inside of the arena, but the side the horse is flexed or bent toward. In the true canter, "inside" corresponds with the inside of the arena (not so in the counter-canter). In the true canter, your inside hand minimally flexes the horse, your inside leg lies at the girth, and your outside leg slightly behind the girth in a "guarding" position. This perfect orchestration of seat, hand, and leg aids keeps the horse in the canter and prevents him from switching leads and breaking into the trot.

An energetic, "uphill" canter.

When a horse tends to push his hindquarters to the inside so he is traveling on two tracks (this tends to happen when reducing speed), it often helps to slightly flex the horse to the outside for one or two canter strides and "catch" the hindquarters by increasing the pressure of your inside leg to prevent this sideways evasion. This realigns the forehand and the hindquarters and thus straightens the horse.

GOAL OF THE MOVEMENT The true canter works well with the horse's natural balance, regardless which pace the gait is ridden, so it is a component of most lower level dressage tests. The counter-canter, on the other hand, is only introduced when the horse begins collected work since it requires a greater amount of balance on the horse's part. Frequent changes between true canter and counter-canter will gymnasticize the horse on both sides of his body, thus promoting "straightness."

FAST FACTS Basic exercise for all phases of riding; can be ridden at all paces (from collected to extended).

PYRAMID FACTOR Rhythm**, relaxation/suppleness**, contact**, impulsion**, straightness**, collection*.

TURN ON THE HAUNCHES

Beginning at the halt, with the horse flexed and bent to the inside, the forehand walks a 180-degree turn around the hindquarters.

HOW IT'S SUPPOSED TO LOOK The correct turn on the haunches begins and ends with the halt, in comparison to the half-turn on the haunches, which is done from the walk or trot (p. 73). The horse should "turn on a plate": imagine you were to put a dinner plate underneath the horse's hind feet. When done correctly, the horse's hind feet will not move off the surface of the plate, but will simply go up and down in the same small area in the regular four-beat walk rhythm.

Individual phases of the turn on the haunches.

The forehand describes a half-circle around the hind legs. The inside hind leg, which forms the pivot and the center of the half-circle, turns on the spot in the rhythm of the movement, while the outside hind leg performs a small circle around the inside one. The horse is bent around the rider's inside leg and also flexed toward the direction of movement—in this case to the inside—and must remain consistently on the aids during the entire turn. Since stepping backward is considered a mistake, a slight forward tendency is desired.

MOST COMMON MISTAKES The Horse: steps backward; stops because one of the hind legs stays "planted" on the ground; pivots (the hind legs stay planted on the ground instead of moving in the walk rhythm); treads a too big "plate" size; evades sideways; crosses hind legs; exhibits too little, or incorrect flexion and bend; goes against the rider's hands.

CORRECT AIDS It is most important to correctly initiate the turn on the haunches because when you err at this stage it is difficult to salvage the movement. From the halt, begin by asking for a step forward. As soon as the horse responds, get his attention with a half-

The horse is being "led" around his haunches, in a controlled manner, step-by-step.

halt, gather him "together," and flex him slightly to the inside while "guiding" him around with your inside hand. At the same time, apply slightly forward-driving pressure with the inside leg at the girth—asking the horse to step around—and leave the outside leg in a "guarding" position. Slightly yield the inside rein. This combination invites the horse to turn around on his haunches.

It's important to maintain flexion and bend until the turn on the haunches is completed—that is, when you are facing the opposite direction, again at the halt. In order to encourage the horse to continue stepping with his hind legs rather than just pivoting around them, you need to keep driving him with your legs and seat; however, you need to contain his forward impulsion with continuous half-halts. Too much hand influence combined with too little pressure from your legs can cause the horse to step backward or stop (both faults), while too much pressure, particularly from the outside leg, can cause the horse to evade sideways or cross his hind legs (also faults).

It's a good idea to draw the turn on the haunches and the position of the

horse's body step-by-step on a piece of paper, and then visualize the turn with your eyes closed. This makes it easier to recognize where you are during the turn on the haunches and thus orchestrate all necessary aids.

GOAL OF THE MOVEMENT The turn on the haunches is a collected movement that allows the rider to change direction in the smallest of spaces. Furthermore, it's a great exercise to improve coordination and concentration in both horse and rider. It also teaches the horse to step under the center of his body with his hind legs, and this, in turn, is an important prerequisite for improving and sustaining work in collection.

FAST FACTS Advanced exercise; suitable for practice during the work phase of a schooling session; improves coordination and "carrying power;" required at Second Level (Elementary in the UK).

PYRAMID FACTOR Rhythm*, relaxation/suppleness*, contact**, impulsion*, straightness*, collection**.

HALF-VOLTE WITH RETURN TO TRACK
An "open" half-circle of 6, 8, or 10 meters in diameter. After completing the half-volte, the horse is ridden diagonally (or obliquely) back toward the track where he started. Always results in a change of direction.

HOW IT'S SUPPOSED TO LOOK A half-volte or half-circle consists of many individual parts: The turn (p. 1), half a volte (p. 171), straightening, and a change of flexion and bend, then re-straightening, which completes the exercise.

In general, a half-volte can be ridden at any given point in the arena. However, you should make a habit of placing it at a precise spot, as the movement is required in dressage tests. If you do it in the second corner of a long side, it is called a "half-volte in the corner with return to track" (p. 24). If you break the movement into its individual components, you release the inside flexion and bend after completing the half-circle, and ride straight on a diagonal at an angle of about 45 degrees back toward the track. As the horse's head reaches the track, briefly change flexion in the poll and bend to the inside to allow the horse the final, shallow turn onto the track. In all of these individual phases the horse must remain consistently on the aids.

MOST COMMON MISTAKES

The Horse: evades with his haunches; gets tense or tight in the turn; returns to the track in a travers-like manner. **The Rider:** turns too early or too late; creates an asymmetrical half-volte; pulls the horse around; rides too steep or too shallow an angle when returning to the track.

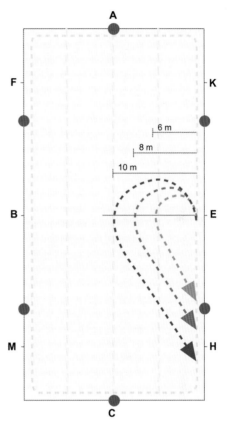

Half-voltes with return to track can be ridden from any given point in the arena.

CORRECT AIDS Riding a correct half-volte with return to the track requires concentration, some skill, spatial sense, and the necessary aids. In detail these are: just before reaching the desired turning point on the long side, give a half-halt on the outside rein to get your horse's attention. At the same time, slightly flex the horse with the inside rein, which you've already shortened a bit, and increase this flexion at the moment you turn. Your inside leg is at the girth, your outside leg slides slightly behind the girth, and the outside rein should yield as much as the inside rein asks for flexion. You must make sure that flexion and bend are even, since only then will you be able to ride on an evenly shaped circle line during the first part of the half-volte.

Once the horse takes on the requested flexion and bend, your inside hand must immediately go forward a bit—that is, "become soft"—in order not to "block" the horse's inside hind leg. You do not want to "pull" the horse around the turn. At the end of the half-circle, slowly release the inside flexion and bend, and slide your outside leg back into its original position at the girth, straightening the horse. In this position, ride the diagonal line back to the track. When reaching the track, give another half-halt and flex the horse slightly to the inside.

This last change of flexion and bend must be done very carefully since the horse is approaching the track at a fairly shallow angle. If you didn't change flexion and bend at all, you would—theoretically— ride right into the arena fence or wall! As soon as the horse's haunches reach the track, release the flexing and bending aids and just ride straight ahead down the long side.

When riding on the diagonal line back to the track, some horses tend to shift their bodies into a travers-like position—especially at the canter. When this happens, it helps to ride a bit more forward—also, slightly flex the horse to the opposite side for a stride, toward the center of the arena. This way the horse should straighten himself again.

GOAL OF THE MOVEMENT Half-voltes with return to the track at the trot are usually only required in lower level dressage tests. They test the rider's aids and the horse's acceptance of these aids. The half-turn with return to track at the canter, required at Second Level (Elementary in the UK) and above, is a way to introduce counter-canter. Like all turns, they also gymnasticize the horse. When schooling, half-voltes can be used as a preliminary step toward working pirouettes (p. 13). In general, half-voltes improve the horse's lateral mobility and increase his ability to take up more weight onto his inside hind leg.

FAST FACTS Basic exercise; can be ridden at collected and working paces, in all three basic gaits; schools coordination, lateral mobility, and "carrying power."

PYRAMID FACTOR Rhythm*, relaxation/suppleness*, contact*, impulsion*, straightness*, collection*.

COUNTER SHOULDER-IN
A shoulder-in ridden on the quarterline (or the inside track), looking toward the arena fence or wall.

HOW IT'S SUPPOSED TO LOOK Unlike the standard shoulder-in (p. 126), the counter shoulder-in is not required in dressage tests and is purely used as a training exercise. Nonetheless, it should be ridden just as rhythmically pure and fluidly, with the horse flexed to the inside and bent around the rider's inside leg. It is not ridden on the track looking toward the center of the arena as in the shoulder-in, but on a parallel track with the horse flexed toward the arena fence or wall. At first sight, this movement might be easily confused with the leg-yield (p. 119) or the travers (p. 145), especially when it's executed incorrectly. Theoretically, the counter shoulder-in can be ridden at all three gaits; however, it's most beneficial at the trot. When cantering, it's better to ride a counter shoulder-fore (p. 129).

MOST COMMON MISTAKES The Horse: exhibits rhythm mistakes; loses impulsion; is too strongly flexed; shows little or no lateral bend; evades through the haunches; tilts his head at the poll.

CORRECT AIDS When you want to ride a counter shoulder-in, ride onto an inside line parallel to the track—the quarterline works well. Then slightly shorten your outside rein (which is now becoming the inside rein) and put a little more weight on your new inside seat bone while determining the amount of flexion you need. The new outside hand yields accordingly, allowing for the necessary stretch in

In this counter shoulder-in, the forehand should be better aligned with the hindquarters so that when observed from the front, you can only see three of the horse's legs.

the muscles on the horse's outer side, and prevents the horse from tilting at the poll. However, do not push the outside rein too far forward since it will cause the horse to evade through his outside shoulder. As soon as the horse is flexed in the new direction, your inside hand must become "light" again to avoid "blocking" the inside hind leg from stepping far underneath the center of the horse's body, and to allow the horse to stretch into the outside rein.

Together with these weight and rein aids, you must apply leg aids: the new inside leg slides slightly behind the girth, and it drives the horse forward-and-sideways, which together with the rider's outside leg, creates the required lateral bend. Your outside leg drives the horse's outside hind leg, asking it to stride forward.

You complete the counter shoulder-in by releasing the flexion, sliding both legs back into their original position and leading the horse's forehand back straight again onto the line. Just as with the beginning of the movement, its finish should proceed smoothly and without overuse of your hands.

Problems with the rhythm and loss of impulsion are best resolved by slightly increasing the pace. If this doesn't work, ride a few strides straight ahead and then begin the movement again. If the counter shoulder-in goes well on a straight line, you can also ride it on bending lines, such as in corners or on a 20-meter circle at "X." This, however, is more difficult since you need to be able to keep the horse's haunches precisely on the line.

GOAL OF THE MOVEMENT The counter shoulder-in is a fantastic way to test the horse's suppleness and "throughness" to the aids on both sides. This exercise also demonstrates just how well the horse actually steps into the outside rein. An alternative to the counter shoulder-in is the counter shoulder-fore, which doesn't require as much lateral bend, and is a great exercise for improving the counter-canter.

FAST FACTS Advanced exercise; level of difficulty can be increased; improves lateral mobility and "carrying power."

PYRAMID FACTOR Rhythm*, relaxation/suppleness*, contact*, impulsion**, straightness***, collection***.

HALF-TURN ON THE HAUNCHES
A 180-degree turn on the haunches where the horse— flexed and bent to the inside and coming from a medium walk or trot—describes an arc that's as small as possible around his hind feet while maintaining the rhythm of the gait, and after the change of direction proceeds again at the medium walk or trot.

HOW IT'S SUPPOSED TO LOOK It can be said the difference between a half-turn on the haunches and a turn on the haunches (p. 65) is that the former is ridden from a medium walk or trot, and the latter from the halt. Just as in the turn on the haunches, the half-turn should be executed "on a plate," meaning that during the turn the horse's front legs step around the hind legs, which describe a very small arc until the horse faces the opposite direction. The horse is bent around the rider's inside leg and flexed in the direction of travel, in this case to the inside. His forefeet and outside hind foot moves around his inside hind, which provides a pivot point and is picked up and put back down slightly in front of where it was before. The transition from walk or trot into the turn and back to the walk or trot out of the turn must be fluid.

In a half turn on the haunches, the horse steps around his hindquarters at the walk.

MOST COMMON MISTAKES The Horse: pauses when initiating the movement; evades sideways with his haunches when initiating movement; crosses his hind legs; stops (plants one hind leg, one or more times); pivots (permanently plants both hind legs); steps backward; treads on a too big "plate"; evades sideways during turn; shows too little flexion and bend; shows incorrect flexion and bend;

loses all flexion and bend; goes against the rider's hand; doesn't move off promptly after the turn.

CORRECT AIDS As with the turn on the haunches, it's very important to initiate the half-turn correctly. After all, you are coming from pure, forward movement—whether big, ground-covering medium walk steps, or the impulsion of the medium trot—and transitioning into a clearly slower movement, where the hind legs must step up and down, rather than forward.

It's helpful to shorten the horse's stride with a half-halt as you slightly flex him to the inside in preparation for the turn. Then, start the turn by "leading" the horse around his hind legs with your inside rein. With your inside leg at the girth, apply a light, forward-driving pressure, while your outside leg helps ask the horse to step around your inside leg, and the supporting outside hand goes forward a bit. Maintain the flexion and bend until the turn is completed—that is, when the horse faces the opposite direction. At that moment, release the flexion, slide your legs back into their original position at the girth to drive the horse forward, and proceed immediately at the walk or trot.

Too much hand combined with too little leg can result in the horse stepping backward during the half-turn, or stopping, both of which are mistakes. It helps to visualize the entire movement step-by-step with your eyes closed prior to riding it.

GOAL OF THE MOVEMENT See turn on the haunches (p. 65). The half-turn helps refine pace differences at the walk since it engages the hindquarters, encourages flexion and bend in the hind joints, and asks the horse to take up more weight behind while his hind legs remain active. Half-turns from the trot help the rider refine her aids.

FAST FACTS Advanced exercise; can be ridden from the medium walk or medium trot; required at Second Level (Elementary in the UK); improves coordination, lateral mobility and "carrying power."

PYRAMID FACTOR Rhythm*, relaxation/suppleness*, contact**, impulsion*, straightness*, collection**.

A half-turn on the haunches as viewed from above.

LATERAL BEND
The combination of flexion and bend from poll to tail through the horse's rib cage.

HOW IT'S SUPPOSED TO LOOK Lateral bend is neither a movement nor an exercise. It is an essential for the horse to be able to complete most school figures and movements with engagement and self-carriage. When a horse is bent laterally, his body is adjusted along its longitudinal axis to exactly overlap the bending line on which he is traveling. This means that if you were looking down on your horse from above, you would see an equal amount of the horse's "body mass" on the right and left side of his longitudinal axis, or the center of the line he is on. The degree of lateral bend is determined by the size and curve of the line or circle. On a big shallow arc such as a 20-meter circle (p. 179), the bend is less pronounced than in a 6-meter volte (p. 171).

MOST COMMON MISTAKES The Horse: exhibits too little or no lateral bend; evades through the hindquarters; falls out through the shoulder; goes against the rider's inside leg; overflexes his neck; tilts his head at the poll. **The Rider:** pulls the horse around with the inside rein.

This horse is clearly bending along his longitudinal axis.

CORRECT AIDS Lateral bending is achieved through correct aids. The best way to do this is to imagine the horse's longitudinal axis from poll to tail as a long, slightly elastic piece of wire. In order to bend this wire, you have to bring the two ends (head and tail) closer together. This can only happen when there is resistance—a post perhaps—in the center to bend the wire around. When riding, this pivotal point is the rider's inside leg, which when positioned at the girth takes on the function of this "post." With the inside rein you flex and position the horse's head (i.e., one end of the wire) to the inside of the bend, while the outside leg is positioned behind the girth to control the haunches (i.e., the opposite end of the wire). All three aid components—inside leg, inside rein, and outside leg—are prerequisites for achieving lateral bend. When one is missing completely, or when one is applied too strongly, correct lateral bend is not possible. Hence, the rider who wants to bend his horse properly must always think of orchestrating all these aids.

GOAL OF THE MOVEMENT Lateral bend is a prerequisite for the functioning of many dressage movements. Only when it's in place can a horse step evenly into both reins (contact), stride with his hind legs precisely in the track of the front legs (straightness), achieve the desired impulsion, and later perform in collection (p. 165). In addition, a horse that moves on a bending line with proper lateral bend is better able to balance himself, thereby taking stress off his ligaments and bones.

A horse should also be bent laterally when on a curve or turning.

FAST FACTS Prerequisite for preserving the horse's soundness; fundamental essential requirement for many dressage movements; improves lateral mobility.

PYRAMID FACTOR Rhythm*, relaxation/suppleness*, contact**, impulsion**, straightness***, collection**.

RISING TROT
A type of seat where the rider alternately sits and rises out of the saddle with the rhythm of the trot.

HOW IT'S SUPPOSED TO LOOK Just as for the sitting trot (p. 28), in the rising trot the rider should be in balance with his horse to avoid disturbing the horse with his seat. The rider rises from the saddle—supported by his stirrups, lower legs, and knees—at the exact moment the horse's inside hind leg swings forward. The rider should perform the rising motion actively and with control so he can adjust to the horse's movement as necessary. The rider must alter his "rising" when the horse's inside hind leg become his outside hind leg as he changes rein or direction. This is known as "changing the

In the rising trot, the rider alternately sits and comes out of the saddle.

diagonal." When the rider has to change the diagonal, he sits two beats instead of one so when riding in the new direction, he is again rising when the horse's inside hind leg swings forward.

MOST COMMON MISTAKES The Rider: is on the "wrong diagonal" (rises when the horse's outside hind leg swings forward); rises too high; exhibits a lack of body control (lets himself be passively "catapulted" out of the saddle); rises and sits out of rhythm of the trot (unintentionally).

CORRECT AIDS Since the rising trot is not really a dressage movement to be learned, there are no special aids for it. Nonetheless, you can and should practice how to do it correctly. A poor rising trot disturbs the horse's motion to quite a degree. When a rider rises too high in the saddle, is too labored, or has too little control over his body, it can help to practice the rising the trot without stirrups. Another excellent exercise for improving your balance and coordination is to rise out of sequence. This means that instead of the usual "rise-sit-rise-sit" in the rhythm of the trot, you "rise-sit-rise-rise-sit-sit-rise," for example. Experienced riders with good body control are able to rise even without stirrups or a saddle!

GOAL OF THE EXERCISE The rising trot tests a rider's body coordination and balance. Furthermore, it should be used in the warm-up and cool-down phases of a schooling session, since it "unburdens" the horse's back, loosening it and preparing it for the sitting trot, or relaxing it after it is tired out from work. The stronger a horse's back muscles are (obtained by adhering to a precise training schedule), the shorter the period you must rise to the trot. For this reason, a young horse is mainly ridden at the rising trot since he will not yet have developed the necessary strength in his back. Riding the sitting trot too early, when the horse's back is still "cold" and tense, makes it more difficult for the rider to sit to the trot motion, thereby causing additional tensions and stresses—a vicious cycle.

FAST FACTS Type of seat at the trot; especially useful for the warm-up and cool-down phase of a schooling session.

PYRAMID FACTOR Rhythm**, relaxation/suppleness**, contact, impulsion*, straightness, collection.

PRAISE AND REWARD
Providing the horse positive reinforcement with the voice, a hand pat or stroke, or treats.

HOW IT'S SUPPOSED TO LOOK Praise and reward should be mandatory—a matter of course. Every rider can decide which way to do it; what matters most is that the horse understands that something pleasurable follows a correct response, good behavior, or extra effort.

MOST COMMON MISTAKES The Rider: doesn't praise or reward at all, or does so only infrequently.

CORRECT AIDS There is no set of aids in this case, just suggestions for how and when to use praise. Using your voice, for example, is something you can do at home, but it's forbidden in a dressage test and is penalized. Treats are also for training sessions only. "Patting" the horse is the only form of praise allowed in the show arena, though it should be less demonstrative than what you might wish to offer at home. In a training session, when a movement has gone well—regardless whether it has just been taught to the horse or it is something he already knows well—you can reward with a generous pat on his neck or his side behind the saddle. Usually, this not only relaxes the horse but the rider, too—which of course has an additional positive effect on the horse. In a similar situation in the show ring, a quiet touch on the horse's neck at the height of his shoulder could recognize his effort in an appropriate manner.

Positive learning

Praise always has a longer-lasting effect than punishment—whether with horse or human. Punishment creates fear, which leads to physical and mental tension, thus preventing learning. When a horse makes a mistake during his work, it is usually because he doesn't understand what is asked—often a result of miscommunication. You should ignore his mistake, repeat the movement and, if necessary, check your aids (are they clear enough and consistent?). When the movement turns out well, you must reward the horse, that is, reinforce him positively. Punishment must only be used when the horse shows obvious undesirable behavior such as biting or kicking—but even then, only used moderately and without anger. As a learning tool, punishment is altogether useless!

GOAL OF THE MOVEMENT It's not just something for "tender-hearted" riders but is supported scientifically: positive reinforcement encourages learning—and shows faster and more lasting success—and helps every rider achieve her aims. Animals do not respond well to punishment during training, and horses are not an exception. In addition, praise and reward improves the horse's state of relaxation, one of the cornerstones of the Training Pyramid.

The rider who wants success—apart from exhibiting an equable demeanor and consistent equestrian skills—should count on giving praise and reward.

FAST FACTS It goes without saying!

PYRAMID FACTOR Rhythm*, relaxation/suppleness***, contact, impulsion, straightness, collection.

Reward and praise—these are a given!

MEDIUM WALK

A pace with a carriage and length of stride between that of the collected and extended walks, where the horse's hind feet step beyond the hoof prints of the front feet.

HOW IT'S SUPPOSED TO LOOK First of all, the rhythm needs to be right: the walk is four beats. A good medium walk is also characterized by the horse's engagement, ground coverage, and the toes of the hind feet stepping beyond the toe-marks of the front. The horse should not move forward with long, sluggish, seesaw-type steps but stride well engaged, with the feet leaving the ground energetically. The horse should be on the aids, drop his neck slightly, and step into the rider's hand so that his nose is slightly in front of the vertical. Only in this position is it possible for the horse to swing his legs out from his shoulders with energy coming over his back while executing even strides with both hind and front legs reaching far forward.

MOST COMMON MISTAKES The Horse: exhibits disturbed rhythm (no clear four-beat rhythm at walk); appears to pace; hurries; is tense; strides short, not reaching "out" from the shoulder enough; shows little to no tracking-up (hind feet barely step into the prints of the front); strides unevenly (walk sequence has one short, then one long stride); jigs; has too little engagement; exhibits inconsistent contact; is above the bit; doesn't stretch forward into the rider's hand; is tight in the neck.

CORRECT AIDS Riding the walk is tricky because many mistakes can creep in unnoticed. Since the inexperienced rider often doesn't feel them, they quickly become habit, which makes them difficult to eliminate. The problem: the walk, unlike the trot and canter, is a gait without impulsion. This makes it impossible to correct faults such as "too little engagement," "tension," or "inconsistent contact" by simply adding a little impulsion.

For this reason, at the walk the rider's aids must be even better orchestrated than at all other basic gaits. This means the coordination of hands, seat, and legs must be just right. It requires you to be in perfect balance and adjust to the movement of the horse's walk—that is, "follow the motion" with your body. This "following" is carried forward all the way into your hands, which allow the natural nodding motion of the horse's head at the walk— caused by the front legs reaching well forward and the resulting movement in the horse's shoulders. Your hands should not remain in place rigidly, but they should not move incessantly, either. They

The rider's hands should follow the nodding of the horse's head in the rhythm of the walk. In combination with seat and leg driving aids, this action allows the horse to reach out further with his legs in medium walk, as seen here.

Nodding motion

The horse's natural nodding motion at the walk is more pronounced the greater the ground coverage, since his shoulder blades (including the base of the neck) have the most up-and-down or forward-and-backward movement in this gait. Also, the horse's balance influences nodding and an unbalanced, young horse often nods more obviously since he still uses his neck as a "balance pole." Quite logically, nodding becomes less pronounced as the steps are shortened, that is, when the degree of collection increases, which only a horse in balance can do, anyway.

should move just slightly forward and backward in the rhythm of the nodding motion. It's not so much a real "movement," but more a gentle "breathing" of the hands and lower arms. Although the reins do slightly affect the horse's frame this way, he can still stretch—a prerequisite for the neck and back muscles to work together.

If the rider has incorrect, "rigid" hands, the horse will permanently tense his back and sooner or later react by showing incorrect or inconsistent rhythm in the walk. For this reason alone, it's *imperative* to smoothly follow the walk motion with your hands. Diagonal driving leg aids support this movement at the walk: at the moment when the horse's left front leg goes forward, increase the pressure with your lower right leg, and when the horse's right front leg goes forward, give the driving aid with your left leg.

When you manage to optimally combine the driving aids of seat and legs with your rein aids sustaining contact, and the horse is stretching into your hand, raising and rounding his back, you can most often improve the quality of the medium walk. Rhythm problems at the walk are best dealt with by riding on bending lines. Also, it's important to always strive for good engagement and relaxation since lack of both also affects rhythm.

GOAL OF THE MOVEMENT The medium walk is the most natural pace at the walk, meaning it's one young horses offer without formal training. From it is developed the collected walk (p. 165) and the extended walk (p. 134). Only when you achieve a correct and quality medium walk early in training can you prevent problems in other paces at the walk. Furthermore, the walk always gives clues about the correctness of training since it exposes deficiencies in contact, "throughness" to the aids, and activity through the horse's back.

FAST FACTS Basic gait; the rider should be able to ask for it at any time with the rhythm always correct.

PYRAMID FACTOR Rhythm*, relaxation/suppleness*, contact*, impulsion, straightness, collection.

MEDIUM TROT

A moderately extended length of stride (between collected and extended) at the trot where the horse's hind feet step further than the horse's front feet.

HOW IT'S SUPPOSED TO LOOK The medium trot is one of the most popular movements considered when deciding for or against a potential dressage prospect. A great medium trot is paramount—everything else is secondary! Is this really true? Of course not. But a spectacular medium trot is even recognized by the layman, and in dressage tests, some judges seem blinded by it, as well. The medium trot, however, is only one of the many pieces of the mosaic that make up a "complete" horse or constitute a well-performed dressage test.

The medium trot is a moderately extended trot stride, in between the collected and extended paces. It should be full of expression, comfortable to sit, with impulsion coming over the horse's back from active hind legs. A clear two-beat rhythm must be maintained throughout. Ideally, at this pace, the horse stretches slightly into the rider's hand, thereby lengthening his frame, with his poll—as it should in almost every movement—remaining the highest point, and his nose at or slightly in front of the vertical.

MOST COMMON MISTAKES The Horse: exhibits inconsistent or incorrect rhythm; hurries; "runs"; has little thrust coming from the hindquarters; is strung out behind; steps wide with his hind legs; breaks into the canter; shows too little change in pace, or doesn't change at all.

CORRECT AIDS At the medium trot, many riders tend to want too much. Instead of staying within the natural abilities of their horse (or his level of training), they "bomb down the highway" no matter what. Most of the time, "less is more," since a harmonious extension generally gets a higher score than a pace that is "overridden" or one that shows an exaggerated action like "toe-flicking." This, of course, doesn't mean that you should always remain at the lower end of the medium trot, but simply that you should adjust what you ask for to your horse's current skill level. When a horse is worked correctly in all paces at the trot, the medium trot can be easily improved since the necessary "pushing" and "carrying power"—the prerequisites for an expressive trot—will be naturally developed.

The medium trot is required from Second Level (Elementary in the UK) onward, though in Young Horse Tests at a later stage. Before this level, where the horse is expected to be "on the bit," we simply speak of "lengthening the stride" (p. 153). In order to be able to perform a correct medium trot, the horse needs to be well balanced.

You can help the horse prepare for this movement by applying half-halts to get his attention before lengthening, slightly gathering him

An expressive trot lengthening: the legs are actively swinging underneath the body.

together and creating greater engagement and activating the hind legs. This is best achieved by applying a "brief pressure" with both lower legs at the same time. The emphasis here is on "brief," since prolonged squeezing won't get you anywhere. In fact, most horses react to it by becoming unwilling and "dead-sided." Therefore, the lower leg must always be used as a momentary driving aid (on and then off the horse's side), never as permanent, lasting pressure.

Because the medium trot is generally ridden across the arena on the diagonal or on the track down the long side you usually have to go through the corner first. This allows you to collect him and get his attention with a half-halt, and the bending line brings his hindquarters under his center of gravity, preparing him for the lengthening of stride. Wait until you have fully negotiated the corner and the horse is completely straight again before you begin the medium trot by moving your hands forward and driving with both legs. Straightening the horse first reduces the risk of the horse mistaking your forward-driving aids for canter aids.

When the medium trot is initiated successfully, the horse will "pull" forward automatically. Ideally, this "pulling"— a sign that the hind legs reach far forward underneath the horse's body, full of impulsion—lasts until the end of the medium trot. The horse's front legs step forward-upward expressively and swing out of the shoulder. It is your job to must sustain all this movement with subtle use of the seat and hand. If you just give the reins forward ("throw them away"), the horse will fall apart and onto his forehand.

To end the medium trot, reduce the length of stride by "gathering" the horse. This is achieved by giving half-halts, restraining with the reins, and at the same time driving the horse's hind legs forward. The increased thrust that was created through the increase in pace is now turned into increased "carrying power" at the reduced pace (whether a working or collected trot). The big movement becomes a smaller one. At the moment the horse responds to the half-halts and

Diagonal and parallel

A medium trot is—like any trot—a movement with a diagonal sequence of footfalls. At least, this is how it's supposed to happen. When taking a closer look, however, you see that this is not always the case, especially during one of those spectacular-looking trot extensions where the diagonal sequence of footfalls is often time-delayed, which—strictly speaking—is a rhythm mistake. An extension is correct when the diagonal leg pairs move in parallel fashion (see photo, p. 86). Imagine two lines drawn through the cannon bones of both front and hind legs as shown in the photo. When the lines are parallel like this, the extension is correct, but when the lines—drawn longer—intersect at some point, the extension is faulty.

"comes back" to you, yield the reins again in order to maintain the
fluidity of the trot.

GOAL OF THE MOVEMENT The medium trot both relaxes and
gymnasticizes the horse, although like many movements, it poses
challenges. It tests the horse's "letting through" of the rider's aids as
well as the rider's influence.

When a horse is bred to be a "sport horse," he should have a certain
degree of athletic ability and movement potential. A medium trot
doesn't have to be spectacular, but it should at least be satisfying, and it
can tell a lot about the horse's "throughness" and quality of training. A
medium trot that has been developed from a loose, "swinging" back
that allows energy to be transmitted through the horse will always be
better than one that is built on tense, rigid muscles. When the latter
occurs, there will be rhythm mistakes, problems with thrust, and
difficulty gathering the horse together in pace transitions.

The medium trot is useful as a means to relax the horse after he's
been ridden in a very collected state, perhaps piaffe (p. 95) or passage
(p. 92), for a long period of time, and using it between such
movements allows any increase in body tension to dissolve (both
"negative" and "positive" body tension).

A medium trot can look different
from one horse to another.

Last but not least, alternating between a medium trot and a collected
or working trot—that is, between increasing and shortening the trot

strides—is a great gymnastic exercise. Going back and forth between "pushing" and "carrying power" strengthens the hindquarters and improves contact.

FAST FACTS Required from Second Level (Elementary in the UK) and Young Horse Tests for five-year-olds onward; develops "pushing power."

PYRAMID FACTOR Rhythm*, relaxation/suppleness*, contact*, impulsion**, straightness, collection.

MEDIUM CANTER
A pace with a length of stride between that of the collected and extended canter, with more uphill balance and more reach than a working pace.

HOW IT'S SUPPOSED TO LOOK Whether you ride at the walk, trot, or canter, the most important characteristic of all three basic gaits is their rhythm. For the canter, this is three beats, which must always be clearly discernible. The medium canter should have an "uphill" tendency and cover more ground each stride than a collected or working pace. Only an extended canter is "larger." The tempo and rhythm should remain the same—it is the ground-covering quality that varies. In a correct medium canter, the horse should stretch slightly more toward the rider's hand, a process that's called "lengthening the frame."

MOST COMMON MISTAKES The Horse: exhibits "shallow" rather than round strides; is hurried; covers little ground; is on the forehand; speeds up; goes against the rider's hand; is crooked (on two tracks).

CORRECT AIDS In a test, all lengthening of gaits, including the medium canter, must be ridden precisely from letter to letter, so the transitions (p. 155) into and out of the extension should be clearly noticeable. This means that after you pass through the corner (medium canter is most often required on the long side or on the diagonal) you increase your forward-driving aids, engaging your back and using your legs, while yielding just enough with your hands so that the horse is able to extend his canter stride without "running away." "Push" your seat in the saddle from back to front in the canter rhythm, thereby supporting the increase in his length of stride. Too much "pushing," however, will cause your upper body to visibly move, which not only looks inelegant but also disturbs the horse's movement.

GOAL OF THE MOVEMENT When you ride the medium canter you "allow" the horse to use more impulsion than is needed for the collected or working canter, so it gives him the opportunity to release energy, and it "freshens" the horse mentally and physically. Also, problems with rhythm in the canter that might arise in training sessions can, most of the time, be eliminated by asking for the medium canter. For this reason, it should always be part of a schooling session.

Frequently changing from medium canter to working or collected canter, is also a good way to gymasticize the horse: he has to take up more weight with his hind legs when he reduces his stride (improving "carrying power"), and when lengthening the canter stride, he has to develop more forward-going strength from his hindquarters (improving "pushing power")—both prerequisites for an expressive canter stride and optimal "jumping through."

FAST FACTS Basic movement; required at Second Level (Elementary in the UK) and above; improves "pushing power."

PYRAMID FACTOR Rhythm**, relaxation/suppleness**, contact**, impulsion**, straightness, collection.

A medium canter covering a lot of ground with "uphill" action.

PASSAGE

A slow and highly cadenced trot where the horse remains airborne during a long moment of suspension.

HOW IT'S SUPPOSED TO LOOK The passage is a high school movement and is accordingly demanding. Like the piaffe (p. 95), it belongs to the group of movements that not all horses are able to perform since it requires, apart from years of systematic and thorough training, a tremendous amount of strength and specific anatomical and physical prerequisites. In the passage, the horse must change his trot motion in such a way so that he trots *less forward* and instead powerfully *upward*, with clear flexion in the haunches, and with hind legs that spring rhythmically forward-and-upward.

The horse swings forward from one pair of diagonal legs to the other, and suspends the pair in the air higher and longer than in the trot. In general, the passage should give the rather complex impression of "powerful lightness." A rider who tries "passage" herself—walking on the ground with slow springy steps, and trying to remain in the air longer between those steps—will get an idea of how much strength and coordination this requires, and might become more patient when teaching her horse the passage!

MOST COMMON MISTAKES The Horse: shows little expression; exhibits little height in suspension; drags his hind legs; simply trots more slowly; has a suspension phase that is only slightly or not at all extended; is not "uphill"; is uneven behind; doesn't show enough angle in hind joints; is strung out behind; is tight in the neck; goes behind the vertical; has a tense back; "hovers"; swishes his tail; sways. **The Rider:** uses too obvious aids; uses whip.

CORRECT AIDS As an introductory note, I'd like to say that the passage is a movement that can be learned by only a few horses—and a few riders, for that matter. This is because the movement requires maximum riding experience, skill, and feel. When incorrect or "coarse" aids are given, a rider can easily overtax the horse and ruin him in the long run. The rider who is not yet quite secure in all riding skills should, therefore, keep her hands off the passage or—should she have the opportunity—learn to ride the movement on a "schoolmaster" that's been very well trained.

The aiding system for the passage begins, like virtually every movement, with a half-halt to signal the horse something new is happening, and to collect him a bit more. Sit vertically and immobile in the center of the saddle so as not to disturb the horse's balance. With both reins, half-halt while evenly driving the horse forward with both legs positioned at or slightly behind the girth. Here, make sure the lower legs are placed somewhat "loosely" on the horse—do not try to "squeeze" the passage out of him. Apart from the fact that this isn't pleasing to the eye, it will also never allow the movement to appear light and expressive, as a passage that's been developed from an active, step-by-step "self-motivating" movement does.

The powerful, springy passage of an eight-year-old horse—here, the hind leg could have been brought slightly more forward.

Depending on whether the passage is developed from the walk or trot, the restraining and driving aids must be attuned to each other accordingly. If it is developed out of the walk, your hand gives a light half-halt and then—almost simultaneously—increases the driving with quick leg aids, then you again half-halt. If it is developed out of the trot, the restraining rein aids are given for longer, while you drive the horse forward at the same time, which causes the trained horse to "compress" more, and expand the airborne phase of suspension. It's very important not to disturb the horse through over-the-top aids but to adjust to his rhythm smoothly.

Experienced riders often ask themselves how to go about developing the first passage steps. There is no recipe that works for all, and depending on a horse's talent, there are different ways that may be best suited to him. For some, it's easier when the rider gathers them from the collected trot, condensing the gait to something approaching half-steps (p. 61). For others, it's easier to do the first steps of passage by bringing the horse back from a trot extension. And, some horses first learn the piaffe, and from that (via half-steps), develop their first passage steps. In any case, it's important that the rider is satisfied initially with just a few passage steps, and doesn't ask for too much, too soon. Overtaxing the horse only leads to mistakes that are difficult to eliminate later.

To prepare for the passage, it has been proven helpful to alternate riding lateral movements, such as shoulder-in (p. 126), travers (p. 145), and renvers (p. 111), since they prepare the horse's hind legs for the more intensive "carrying" action to come.

GOAL OF THE MOVEMENT A high school movement—at least in today's dressage world—the passage is virtually an end in itself. It's the goal of many dressage riders, or at least a large part of it. And yet, the passage can positively influence other areas of a horse's training. For example, it is on the path to developing the passage that the quality of the basic trot improves most. Even horses with a rather normal, unimpressive gait, who through talent and hard work learn to passage, will in the end often demonstrate clearly better trot mechanics overall.

FAST FACTS Very advanced movement; high degree of difficulty that increases when performed on a bending line or in the half-pass (p. 148); requires "pushing power" and a huge amount of strength ("carrying power").

PYRAMID FACTOR Rhythm, relaxation/suppleness, contact*, impul-
sion**, straightness, collection***.

PIAFFE
A cadenced trot on the spot, where the horse steps from one diagonal pair of legs to the other with a moment of suspension.

HOW IT'S SUPPOSED TO LOOK In the piaffe—like the passage (p. 92), it's a high school dressage movement—the horse should step diagonally on the spot. Between the diagonal leg pairs leaving the ground there should be a brief moment of free suspension. Ideally, the horse's front lower legs are each lifted so they "hang" vertically momentarily before they are lowered again. The haunches are lowered as the hind legs clearly take up the horse's weight, and his back should "swing." Each hind leg should leave the ground and be lifted up until the hoof reaches approximately the height of the fetlock joint of the other (the weight-bearing) leg.

At Grand Prix, the horse is allowed to move forward one to two hoof widths during the piaffe, and in Intermediaire II tests, up to a meter. The rider sits as quietly as possible. It should look as if the horse is almost piaffing on his own.

MOST COMMON MISTAKES The Horse: piaffes unevenly; "rakes" the ground with his feet; "plants" one or more feet on the ground; steps backward (entire horse or only one hind leg); steps wide behind; steps wide in front; sways; has a high croup; lifts his hind hooves too high (higher than his front hooves); doesn't take up weight with his hindquarters; appears to "hop"; is tight in the neck; goes behind the vertical; sticks his tongue out; has a tense back; swishes his tail; goes against the rider's hand; disobeys. **The Rider:** overuses aids (too much whip, spurs, voice).

"Pi" or "Pa"— what comes first?

"As a basic principle, I generally develop piaffe first. From a correct piaffe carried by the haunches, develops the transition into the passage, and thereby the passage itself. However, there's no rule without exception. When horses offer the passage naturally, you can school the passage first, and from it, develop the piaffe. What's important is that the horse works increasingly from his hindquarters. A horse's natural talent to passage, however, must not be confused with 'hovering' steps since they are the result of slow, inactive hind legs with the horse tense in the back, strong in the hand, and not developing 'springing' power. Passage, on the other hand, is characterized by the horse propelling himself off the ground making the phase of suspension last longer."

KLAUS BALKENHOL
Olympic medalist, World Champion, former trainer of the U.S. Olympic dressage team

CORRECT AIDS To ride a correct (and beautiful) piaffe is not easy. It's important—just as with passage—that only a rider who's skilled and experienced should attempt it. The horse must already have achieved consistent "straightness" and collection, and he should let the rider's aids "through." Sometimes, a young horse is asked to "step in place" as part of an early assessment of his talents, but this has nothing to do with "real" piaffing since such a horse hasn't acquired the necessary physical and mental prerequisites. When, on the other hand, a horse has already been trained in collection to a such a degree that he "compresses" at the lightest of aids, lowering his haunches on cue, he can begin seriously schooling the piaffe.

As always, begin by getting the horse's attention with half-halts, while bracing your back slightly more, though this should be done without sitting more heavily. The tendency here must be to burden the horse's back *less*, not more. Drive the horse's hind legs forward by simultaneously and equilaterally giving brief aids with both your legs, and "gathering" the movement step-by-step by giving half-halts.

At this point, you should take the following to heart:
1: Initially, be satisfied with two or three piaffe-like steps.
2: Disturb the horse and his balance as little as possible.

The horse must learn your aids for the piaffe, which might seem somewhat odd—even confusing—to him at first, and learn to coordinate his movements accordingly. Most of the time early in training, you can't expect to piaffe for many steps. When the rider is content with "just a little" initially, the horse usually understands what is being asked of him more quickly, and is more willing to try.

The same policy holds true for applying the piaffe aids: less is always more! When the piaffe is achieved through "hitting" and "poking" (in such cases, we can't say it is being properly "developed"—merely forced), the poorer the representation of the piaffe will be—that is, if it's achieved at all. When you see a horse that was "trained" to piaffe in this manner, you might grimly define the movement as "angst on the spot." And this, of course, is exactly what it should *not* be.

A correctly trained horse that is physically and mentally prepared and positioned to execute the piaffe will do so without fear and almost on his own, making overly obvious or forceful aids completely unnecessary.

GOAL OF THE MOVEMENT While the passage commonly has a positive "side effect" of improving a horse's basic trot, the piaffe is an end in itself. It's the crowning achievement of correct, progressive collective work—and, in a sense, the icing on the cake. Along the way, it improves strength in the horse's hindquarters.

FAST FACTS Very advanced movement; required at Intermediaire II and Grand Prix; requires strength, endurance, and a great amount of coordination.

PYRAMID FACTOR Rhythm*, relaxation/suppleness*, contact*, impulsion*, straightness, collection***.

This horse's piaffe, who at the time of the photo shoot was still at the beginning of his Grand Prix career, is already quite expressive.

A canter pirouette.

PIROUETTE

Collected turn on the horse's haunches at the walk (walk pirouette) or at the canter (canter pirouette).

HOW IT'S SUPPOSED TO LOOK I distinguish between walk and canter pirouettes: walk pirouettes are required at Third Level (Medium/ Advanced Medium in the UK) and above, canter pirouettes at Fourth Level (Advanced in the UK) and above. Since they do not look the same and involve different aids, I'd like to explain them separately.

Walk Pirouette It resembles the half-turn on the haunches (p. 73); however, it is ridden exclusively out of the collected walk so has a higher degree of collection and smaller arc in its 180-degree turn. The prerequisite for a successful walk pirouette is proficiency in both the turn on the haunches (p. 65) and the half-turn on the haunches. In the walk pirouette, the horse should maintain a shortened four-beat rhythm of the walk. The horse treads a half-circle around his haunches with his forehand, moving with his outside hind leg around the inside hind leg, which should rhythmically leave and touch the ground. The horse is flexed and bent in the direction of travel.

The individual phases of a canter pirouette.

Canter Pirouette These are both *half* and *full* pirouettes. The half pirouette describes a path of 180 degrees, the full pirouette a circle of 360 degrees. Half and full pirouettes are always ridden at the collected canter. The horse's forehand, flexed and bent in the direction of travel, "jumps" around the haunches in a circle, while the inside hind leg moves on an arc that's as small as possible. The haunches should lower and take up more of the horse's weight. During the entire pirouette, the three-beat rhythm of the canter must be clearly recognizable. For a half pirouette, a horse needs three or four canter strides, and for a full pirouette, six to eight. Before, during, and after the pirouette, the horse should not leave the straight line on which he is cantering.

MOST COMMON MISTAKES

Walk Pirouette **The Horse:** pauses before beginning movement; evades sideways with his hindquarters; "stops" ("plants" one or more legs firmly on the ground); pivots ("plants" both hind legs and swings around them); steps backward; is not centered; uses too much ground; crosses his hind legs; evades sideways during turn; loses rhythm; shows too little flexion and bend; is incorrectly flexed and bent; goes against the rider's hand; exhibits a "flat" or "shallow" turn.

A clear three-beat rhythm must be maintained at every phase of the canter pirouette.

Canter Pirouette **The Horse:** "throws" himself around his hind legs; begins in a travers-like manner; evades sideways; uses too much ground; loses rhythm; bears little weight on his hind end; steps simultaneously with both hind legs; loses impulsion; labors; exhibits little lateral bend; is incorrectly flexed and bent; is tight in the neck; goes against the rider's hand; shows resistance.

CORRECT AIDS

Walk Pirouette First of all, apply half-halts to prepare the horse for the new task ahead. Almost simultaneously, slightly flex the horse to the inside, increase your weight on the inside seat bone and activate the horse's inside hind leg using the inside leg at the girth. Your outside leg is positioned in a slight "guarding" position behind the girth, bending the horse around your inside leg and preventing the haunches from falling out. The orchestration of seat, leg, and rein aids controls the turn, whereby the inside rein not only flexes the horse but also guides him sideways.

After completing the walk pirouette, release the flexion and bend, drive the horse forward using seat and leg aids while yielding with the hand at the same time. If a horse tends to not move his hindquarters in the rhythm of the movement, begin by riding the

pirouette a bit larger and more forward. Sideways evasion of the haunches can be best prevented by asking the horse for less flexion and bend, if necessary by riding a few steps in counter-flexion.

Canter Pirouette Regardless whether you ride a half or full canter pirouette, you initiate it the same way. In both cases you "gather" the horse a little more, meaning you increase collection by giving a few half-halts. Then you apply all the necessary aids for the canter.

At the same time, increase your weight on the inside seat bone, and flex the horse a bit more to the inside. While using the inside rein to guide the canter movement sideways, your inside leg at the girth maintains the horse's bend in the rib cage and activates his inside hind leg. Your outside leg is positioned behind the girth, keeping the hindquarters in place and bending the horse around your inside leg.

Your inside hand must continuously be light in order not to block the horse's inside hind leg. "Give" the outside rein slightly forward to allow for the bend; however, you must keep enough contact to prevent the horse from evading through his outside shoulder.

In the pirouette, the horse's hindquarters should describe an arc that is as small as possible.

Continue to give all canter aids, similar to when cantering on. When

Important! Don't overdo work on pirouettes

"A prerequisite for beginning work on canter pirouettes is good collection. With young horses, that is, six-year-olds, I prepare pirouettes from collection of the canter 'jump' in shoulder-in. The horse must be able to canter 'on a plate' for a series of steps, whereby rhythm and impulsion must be maintained. When this is accomplished, I set the horse up for two or three pirouette jumps. Initially, I don't worry about the size, but more about whether or not the horse clearly jumps through and moves evenly and easily around his own axis. I gradually decrease the size. Many riders begin pirouettes by way of riding travers at the canter. I prefer using the shoulder-in or the shoulder-fore. This way, the inside hind leg has more distance to cover, making the risk of his changing leads or 'jumping parallel' much less. It's also highly important not to overdo work on pirouettes since the hocks can get stressed. With younger horses, I ride two or three pirouettes at the walk, but not daily. With older horses, I sometimes don't ride pirouettes for days, and only when getting them ready for a test. What's more important is a rider's all-encompassing collected work. It creates the 'letting through of the aids' and is the best preparation. A horse that comes back to the rider well during collection usually has no problems with pirouettes."

ISABELL WERTH
Olympic medalist, World Champion, European Champion, World Cup winner

riding a horse that's been trained correctly at pirouettes, it is often enough just to flex the horse with the inside hand, while riding the turn itself rather "on" the outside rein. Just before completing the pirouette—that is, either a half circle or a full circle—gradually straighten the horse again and drive him forward out of the pirouette using seat and leg aids.

The "straighter" a horse is, the better his pirouettes will be—both to the left and right. Nonetheless, if the horse tends to have bigger problems in one direction, for example, "throwing" himself against the rider's inside leg, it's helpful to step back and go back to riding working pirouettes for a while (p. 13).

GOAL OF THE EXERCISE

Walk Pirouette A collected movement that can be used to change direction in the smallest of spaces. Walk pirouettes are also, just like the turn on the haunches and the half-turn on the haunches, a great exercise to improve coordination and concentration in both horse and rider. Furthermore, the horse continuously brings himself underneath his center of gravity with his hind feet, a process that furthers "loftiness" and elevation—even in the collected walk.

Canter Pirouette This movement is a requirement at Fourth Level (Advanced in the UK) and its level of difficulty must not be underestimated. It also tests the rider's aiding ability and the horse's level of training. Furthermore, when developing canter pirouettes—that is, doing preparatory collected work—you are also improving the "carrying power" of the haunches at the canter, and thus ultimately, collection at the canter.

After completing the canter pirouette, the rider continues by riding straight again.

The increased flexion in the haunches and their "taking up" more of the horse's weight stresses the horse's joints and muscles. Although this work will help the muscles to strengthen in the long run, when first schooling pirouettes you should be satisfied with just a few strides, and only increase your demands slowly. Otherwise, muscle fatigue could lead to mistakes, and eventually, resistance, jeopardizing the horse's health and the learning process.

FAST FACTS

Walk Pirouette Required at Third Level (Medium/Advanced Medium in the UK) and above; advanced movement.

Canter Pirouette Required at Fourth Level (Advanced in the UK) and above; advanced to high level of difficulty; requires great amount of coordination and "carrying power."

PYRAMID FACTOR Rhythm, relaxation/suppleness, contact, impulsion*, straightness, collection**.

A turn in the square volte.

SQUARE VOLTE
A misleading term for a preparatory exercise to the pirouette—ridden on a square.

HOW IT'S SUPPOSED TO LOOK The term "square volte" is really a paradox. A volte (p. 171) is perfectly round; a square has four edges. Somehow these don't fit together! However, I'd like to keep the name as it is since it's still commonly used.

Often in the middle of the arena, you ride a square with sides that are roughly the same length (see diagram, p. 109). In each corner of the square, you ride a quarter-pirouette around the horse's inside hind leg. From there, you ride straight toward the next corner of the square, perform another quarter-pirouette in that corner, and so on. It is ridden at the walk and canter only.

MOST COMMON MISTAKES The Horse: is crooked along the sides of the square; goes against the rider's inside leg in the corners; falls out with his haunches in the corners; exhibits rhythm mistakes; pivots ("plants" both hind legs); "throws" himself around his hind end. **The Rider:** doesn't position the horse's hindquarters properly in the corners.

CORRECT AIDS The aids are somewhat different, depending on whether the square volte is ridden at the walk or canter. At the walk, the horse begins on a straight line. Just before the first corner of your imaginary square, slightly flex the horse to the inside. Now lead the horse with the inside rein into a 90-degree turn and add a bit more weight to your inside seat bone while at the same time applying pressure with the inside leg at the girth. The outside leg is positioned behind the girth to keep the hindquarters in place. This way, you guide the horse around a quarter-pirouette in two or three steps, then ride straight ahead on the next straight line of the square by releasing flexion and bend, and driving with both legs at the girth.

At the canter, the aids are similar; however, you sit more on your inside seat bone. When beginning the quarter-volte, you must increase your weight shift slightly more emphatically than you would at the walk, and then you return to center after the turn.

GOAL OF THE MOVEMENT Riding square voltes increases the horse's obedience to the rider's legs. The horse learns to accept the rider's inside leg instead of simply "throwing" himself sideways into the turn. Square voltes are not a "must" in training, however, they are a great exercise to prepare the horse for walk and canter pirouettes later on, and also a great corrective exercise if and when pirouettes go wrong.

FAST FACTS Exercise for the work phase of a schooling session; can be ridden at various degrees of collection; ridden at walk and canter only; builds strength; schools obedience to leg.

PYRAMID FACTOR Rhythm*, relaxation/suppleness*, contact*, impulsion*, straightness**, collection**.

Riding school figures correctly

"Riding school figures and movements accurately in dressage tests helps you to earn points. This is not just because they look nicer or conform to a certain pattern, rather, riding them successfully gives judges information about the way the horse is ridden and about the control the rider has over him. Furthermore, only through accuracy can you achieve the desired gymnastic effect of an exercise. Circles that have edges or are egg-shaped show, for example, that the horse is not completely on the outside rein, lateral bend is missing, and he is pressing against the rider's inside leg. And, these misshaped circles render the purposes of riding a circle— improving lateral mobility in the muscles and increased weight-bearing from the inside leg—useless. Only when the rider remains exactly on the line of a school figure, at every step, stride or jump, can you give the aids that will lead to systematic work with the horse—instead of merely rattling off movements."

HEINER SCHIERGEN
Grand Prix rider and trainer

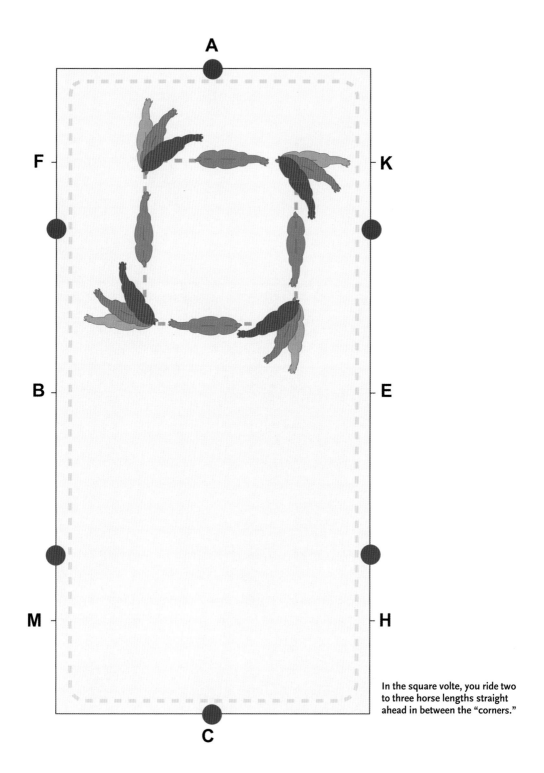

In the square volte, you ride two to three horse lengths straight ahead in between the "corners."

Renvers: The horse moves on four tracks, and his front and hind legs cross. In this photo, I would have preferred the poll to be slightly higher.

RENVERS (HAUNCHES-OUT)

A forward-and-sideways (lateral) movement where the horse is flexed and bent in the direction of travel, with his haunches on the track while his forehand is led toward the center of the arena on an inside track.

HOW IT'S SUPPOSED TO LOOK The renvers is best imagined as a shoulder-in (p. 126) in counter-flexion (and with counter-bend). It is also the "mirror image" of the travers (p. 145). Like all lateral movements (p. 76), it must be ridden with enough of a "forward tendency."

The horse is flexed to the inside and bent around the rider's inside leg: remember that here, as with the counter-canter, "inside" doesn't refer to the inside of the arena but to the "shortened," bent, or flexed side of the horse. Going on, the renvers is ridden with the haunches on the track, and the forehand on an inside track toward the center of the arena at about a 30-degree angle from the rail. The horse is bent toward the track and the direction he is traveling. The renvers is correct when its execution is smooth and fluid, there is a steady rhythm and lots of impulsion, and the horse is continuously on the aids.

Renvers is ridden, like travers, on four tracks. The horse's legs should reach out and cross each other as much as possible. Renvers can also be ridden at the walk, trot, and possibly at the counter-canter, usually at a collected pace. Do note, however, that in order to prevent loss of impulsion, you may need to occasionally (and temporarily) increase to a working gait.

MOST COMMON MISTAKES The Horse: shows too much or too little flexion; falls out through the outside shoulder; has too little lateral bend; is incorrectly flexed and bent; exhibits rhythm mistakes; is crooked; deviates from the line of the exercise; loses impulsion; hurries; labors; goes against the rider's hand; is tight in the neck; tilts his head at the poll. **The Rider:** begins the movement too abruptly.

CORRECT AIDS It's best to initiate renvers after passing through the corner, though it can begin at any point on the long side of the arena. It's helpful to imagine beginning a one-loop or two-loop serpentine (p. 122), or a shoulder-in. Similar to riding serpentines or a shoulder-in, lead the horse's forehand away from the track at an angle, then immediately "gather" the horse with the "new" outside rein, flex the horse toward the fence or wall, and put more weight onto your "new" inside seat bone. While you do this, slide the formerly inside (now outside) leg behind the girth into a "guarding position"—thereby keeping the haunches on, and driving them along, the track. At the same time, your new inside leg applies more pressure at the girth and asks the horse's new inside hind leg to step more forward. Through the combination of the forward-and-sideways driving aids, the horse—flexed and bent—will move forward-and-sideways on a straight line, roughly at a 30-degree angle from the rail.

To make this clearer: if, for example, you are about to come down the long side of the arena on the left rein, after passing through the corner, flex and bend the horse to the right. The forehand will move away from the track while the haunches remain on it. As you come to the end of the long side, slowly release flexion and bend and lead the horse's forehand back onto the track. The formerly outside leg now becomes the inside leg again, which helps you keep the horse's hindquarters on the track and prevent them from suddenly swinging sideways toward the center of the arena.

If this sounds complicated, that's because it is! This is why the renvers is not required before Second Level (Elementary in the UK). To prevent loss of impulsion, which is usually a result of too much hand and too little forward-sideways driving seat and leg aids, the movement shouldn't just be ridden in a collected pace but also at a working pace once in a while. This way you can maintain the "freshness" of the movement, and avoid many a mistake.

GOAL OF THE MOVEMENT Like all lateral movements, renvers is an excellent exercise for improving the horse's "carrying power" and, subsequently his letting the aids "through" and collection, since his inside hind leg is repeatedly asked to step more underneath his center of gravity. At the same time, as a lateral exercise, it gymnasticizes the horse very effectively in his trunk and neck muscles: the horse's muscles are "shortened" on the inside while those on the outside are stretched. Therefore, frequently changing from renvers to the left and renvers to the right, combined with shoulder-in and travers, is a very valuable exercise for the entire horse's body, as well as improving the rider's coordination in general. Alternating between renvers, travers, and shoulder-in is very popular among experienced trainers when preparing the horse for the piaffe (p. 95) and passage (p. 92).

This is how renvers looks from above.

FAST FACTS Advanced movement; increased level of difficulty; required at Second Level (Elementary in the UK); improves lateral mobility; builds strength.

PYRAMID FACTOR Rhythm*, relaxation/suppleness*, contact**, impulsion**, straightness**, collection***.

REIN-BACK

The horse moves backward in a two-beat, diagonal sequence of footfalls. The rein-back is either followed by a halt or a transition to the walk, trot, or canter.

HOW IT'S SUPPOSED TO LOOK When executing a rein-back, the horse should step backward calmly and relaxed in a straight line at the rider's request. Like the trot, the rein-back is a diagonal movement. It should look as if the horse is lifting his diagonal leg pairs simultaneously, stepping back and then stepping down again with these two legs at the same time. The poll should remain the highest point, and the horse should "let the aids through," actively back off the bit, and willingly halt (p. 58) or go forward again on command. The rider is either required to perform a certain number of steps (commonly four, five, or six) or is asked to "rein-back a horse's length," which is about three or four steps.

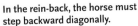

In the rein-back, the horse must step backward diagonally.

When the rein-back is finished with a halt, the horse's last step should move all four legs evenly underneath his body so he's standing square. If the requirement is to walk, trot, or canter on following the rein-back, the forward movement should develop directly from the backward movement without hesitation. This combination of backward-forward-backward is sometimes called a "seesaw" (p. 118).

MOST COMMON MISTAKES The Horse: does not display diagonal movement; is crooked; "creeps" back (is too slow or low energy); rushes or hurries; goes against the rider's hand; is tight in the neck; exhibits little or no "throughness" to the aids; is resistant; halts not square after rein-back; hesitates when transitioning forward out of rein-back.

CORRECT AIDS In order to perform the rein-back, apply—as you must before virtually every movement—a half-halt to "get the horse's attention." Your upper body should incline slightly forward to "unburden" the horse's back, and both lower legs should be a little behind the girth.

At the beginning of the rein-back, apply a brief go-forward aid with your legs to ask the horse to move. (With many horses, it's helpful to apply the leg pressure not from the calves, but from the knees, and put

your lower legs only loosely on the horse's sides.) At the very moment the horse responds and lifts a leg, restrain him with both reins, and transform the developing forward movement into a backward movement. As soon as the horse brings one foot backward, soften your hand. This is the way to continue with the movement, step-by-step.

Complete the rein-back by repositioning your legs at the girth, sitting more "heavily" again, and releasing the restraining rein aids.

When, after the rein-back, you ask for a halt, the horse's last step should squarely line up his front and hind leg pairs—in other words, it's a half-step. When, on the other hand, you ask the horse to walk, trot, or canter on from the rein-back, ride forward immediately without pause.

The sign of a well-ridden, well-trained horse is when only the slightest of aids are sufficient to execute a rein-back. When riding one that is less trained, you should be careful to *never* try to pull him backward with force. The rein-back is the only movement that's truly not at all natural for a flight animal like the horse. When he senses danger ahead of him, a horse would rather veer away and run off than move backward! For this reason, the rein-back requires a great amount of trust between horse and rider. If you simply "pull" the horse backward rather than *ride* him back, he'll always resist your hand, tense his back, and, if he backs up at all, step back unwillingly and incorrectly.

Problems with the rein-back are best resolved from the ground. This means, dismounting, standing next to the horse's shoulder, and "explaining" to the horse how to back up by applying slight pressure with the reins, possibly supported by lightly touching him with the whip (on the front legs or the point of shoulder), and by using your voice. If an assistant is available, you can do this exercise when mounted with your helper applying the additional aids on the ground.

GOAL OF THE MOVEMENT The rein-back is quite a multilayered movement. It gives valuable clues to the level of trust, relaxation, and "throughness to the aids" in a horse. And, it also improves, when ridden correctly, overall "throughness" and collection, since the horse has to bend or "angle" his hindquarters and hind legs in a very pronounced way, taking up more of his weight. Trot-to-halt-to-rein-back, combined with trotting off again, has a similar gymnastic and strength-building effect for horses that knee bends have for humans.

In this rein-back the rider is clearly slightly lightening her seat and sliding her lower legs back.

FAST FACTS Basic exercise; can be ridden at the end of warm-up and in the work phase of a schooling session; improves coordination and "carrying power."

PYRAMID FACTOR Rhythm, relaxation/suppleness*, contact*, impulsion*, straightness, collection**.

The measure of relaxation

"It's crucial that a horse backs up from the rider's leg and not from the rider's hand. Many a rider makes the mistake of trying to pull his horse backward with too much hand influence. This results in the horse tensing his back, leaning against the reins and not stepping backward diagonally. If, on the other hand, you influence the horse with a light hand and clear leg aids, you will be able to control the movement step-by-step. The rein-back is a measurement of relaxation and a movement that can be perfected with refined aids and well-rated practice."

MICHAEL KLIMKE
Grand Prix rider, German dressage champion

SEESAW

Beginning at the halt, the seesaw is a combination of moves: rein-back to walk forward to rein-back followed by walking, trotting, or cantering on.

HOW IT'S SUPPOSED TO LOOK The seesaw is always ridden from the halt, with a specified number of steps. Initially, the horse stands squarely, then performs a rein-back (p. 114), followed by riding forward for the required number of steps, and then another rein-back. You complete the seesaw by walking, trotting, or cantering off (pp. 8, 10, and 5). The entire movement, including the exit, must be performed smoothly and fluidly. The horse must not come to a stop in-between. During the rein-back, the horse must maintain a clear two-beat rhythm, and when riding forward at the walk, a clear four-beat rhythm, and when at the trot or canter, a two-beat or three-beat, respectively. Since the seesaw doesn't result in a halt, there are no half-steps necessary to achieve a square halt (as in the rein-back followed by a halt—p. 114.)

MOST COMMON MISTAKES The Horse: hesitates; is not fluid; does not display diagonal movement; steps wide behind; is crooked; exhibits little to no "throughness" to the aids; "runs" backward; is tight in the neck; comes behind the bit; goes against the rider's hand. **The Rider:** backs the horse too few or too many steps; "pulls" the horse backward.

CORRECT AIDS The aids for the seesaw are a combination of aids for the rein-back and walking, trotting, and cantering. To be able to ride the movement with fluidity requires concentration and feel from the rider, and an advanced level of "throughness" from the horse. The number of steps is specified. When, for example, it's "4-4-4," you have to ride four steps backward, four steps forward, and another four steps back, before walking, trotting, or cantering off.

The rider applies the aid for the forward movement at the moment the horse lifts his last diagonal pair in the final step of the rein-back.

And, when changing from the forward movement into the second rein-back, you "gather" the horse during the final step forward, transforming it instead into a step back. To avoid a situation where the horse starts to anticipate the number of steps backward and forward—and go ahead on his own prior to your request—it's helpful to vary the number every now and then. Only then can you be sure to keep control of the seesaw exercise.

GOAL OF THE MOVEMENT Because it is a combination of two different rhythms—the two-beat of the rein-back and the four-beat of the walk forward—the seesaw requires the horse be collected and well ridden. For this reason, the way a horse performs this exercise informs the rider, trainer, and ultimately, a judge about the degree of the horse's "throughness"—the goal of dressage training in the first place.

FAST FACTS Advanced movement; requires collection; can be ridden in the work phase of a schooling session; improves coordination and both "carrying" and "pushing power."

PYRAMID FACTOR Rhythm, relaxation/suppleness, contact, impulsion, straightness, collection*.

LEG-YIELDING

A forward-and-sideways (lateral) movement where the horse is flexed (but not bent) against the direction of travel and his inside front and hind legs cross in front of his outside legs.

HOW IT'S SUPPOSED TO LOOK Leg-yielding, closely related to leg-yielding away from and back to the track (p. 169), is required in First Level dressage tests (Novice in the UK) and is also a popular exercise used to prepare young horses for the half-pass (p. 148). In dressage tests, leg-yielding is only required at the walk; however, it can also be ridden at the trot. In either case, the horse must remain in the rhythm of the respective gait, maintaining tempo.

When you leg-yield along the track, you can do so either with the horse's head toward the arena fence or wall, or his tail toward the fence or wall. For example's sake, when the horse's head is flexed toward the wall, his forehand stays on the track, and his hindquarters move toward the center of the arena at a roughly 45-degree angle to the track. When you ride on the left rein, the horse yields to the right leg. Note: in the leg-yield, the horse is *flexed* not *bent*.

MOST COMMON MISTAKES The Horse: loses rhythm; labors; drags his feet; is overflexed; deviates from the line of travel (track); goes against the rider's hand; is tight in the neck. **The Rider:** drives the horse too much sideways and not enough forward, or vice versa.

CORRECT AIDS Leg-yielding can be done across a diagonal to a specified point on the rail, or along the track in the two positions I mentioned earlier. To initiate a leg-yield, flex the horse *away* from the direction he will be traveling—toward the leg from which he is yielding. If, for example, you are riding along the track, flex the horse toward the fence or wall while positioning your leg on that side (now the "inside") behind the girth, pushing the haunches toward the center of the arena. With this leg, you drive the horse along the track forward-and-sideways. The leg on the opposite side (the "outside") remains in a more forward position, absorbing the sideways movement, thus preventing the hindquarters from swinging around too far. At the end of the line along which you intend to leg-yield, align the horse's haunches with the forehand by sliding both your legs back into their original position, and straighten the horse.

In all the lateral exercises, the forward movement must always be more pronounced than the sideways movement.

GOAL OF THE EXERCISE At the beginning of their training, horses must learn a few basic aids: those for forward, backward, halting, and going sideways. In this respect, the leg-yield is the first exercise that teaches the horse to understand sideways driving aids and respond promptly to them.

Going sideways is a prerequisite for any type of riding. Furthermore, the leg-yield is a great exercise that gymnasticizes the horse laterally without putting too much stress on the joints, since the horse's legs don't cross as far and the hind legs don't have to take up as much weight as in other lateral movements. For this reason, leg-yielding can be ridden at a working trot and can also be used as a warm-up exercise.

FAST FACTS Basic movement; can be ridden in the warm-up and work phase of a schooling session; improves coordination.

PYRAMID FACTOR Rhythm*, relaxation/suppleness**, contact**, impulsion*, straightness**, collection.

Leg-yielding along a diagonal line.

SERPENTINES

Leaving the track on specified bending lines at the walk, trot, or canter. There are four types of serpentines: double-loop; single-loop; along the centerline; and across the arena.

HOW IT'S SUPPOSED TO LOOK All four types of serpentines should be demonstrated, regardless of the gait, with a clear rhythm and even tempo, as well as with flexion and bend. Since serpentines go back and forth across the arena, you must change flexion and bend every time you change direction. During these changes the horse should remain in light contact and securely on the aids, and his body's longitudinal axis should adjust smoothly to each bending line (lateral bend). Serpentines are ridden in the basic gaits at the working and collected paces.

Single-Loop Serpentine This is ridden along the long side of the arena and goes from one corner into the next (see diagram, p. 123). After passing through the first corner onto the long side, turn your horse at the first letter and ride in a shallow curve toward the center of the quarterline so that the outermost point of the serpentine is 5 meters from the track. When you reach this point, change flexion and bend, and ride toward the letter at the end of the same long side, where you again change flexion and bend as you reach the track.

In dressage tests, the single-loop serpentine is commonly ridden at the rising and sitting trot (pp. 77 and 28). If you perform it at a rising trot, you must change diagonal first just as you get to the middle of the serpentine, and again at the end—that is, whenever you change flexion and bend. Use the same points for lead changes (simple, p. 41, and flying, p. 45) when cantering.

Double-Loop Serpentine The path of the double-loop serpentine starts along the long side, and its two loops extend to approximately 2 1/2 meters away from the track (see diagram, p. 124). First turn onto the long side and immediately ride at an angle toward the half-quarterline, there change flexion and bend, and ride toward the middle of the long side (i.e., toward "B" or "E"). Upon arrival, change flexion and bend again, turn, and ride the second curve like the first one. The double-loop serpentine is ridden at the sitting trot. It can also be ridden at the walk. It's less suited for the canter since the rider has to turn, and change flexion and bend multiple times in quick succession.

Serpentine Along the Centerline In this special type of serpentine, start in the middle of the short side of the arena, as if riding a 10-meter volte (see diagram, p. 124). After riding a quarter-volte, you arrive at the quarterline (5 meters away from the track on the long side), and from there ride back across the centerline toward the quarterline on the opposite side. Repeat, again riding back across the centerline to the opposite quarterline, and finally toward the middle of the short side. The centerline is crossed twice, and with every change of direction you must adjust the horse's flexion and bend to the new line.

A single-loop serpentine

Serpentine Across the Arena As its name suggests, in this serpentine, the loops lead across the entire arena (see diagram, p. 125). You begin and end this serpentine in the middle of the short sides. Throughout the movement, the size of the loops depends on the number of them ridden: in a 40-meter arena, for example, you can ride three to four serpentines; in a 60-meter arena, more.

After exiting the corner of the long side, turn and ride parallel to the short side across the arena toward the opposite long side. There, turn

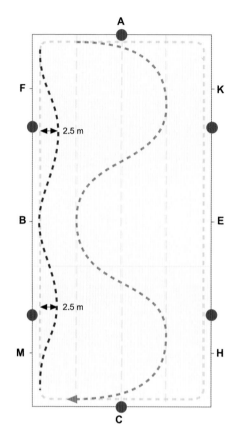

A double-loop serpentine and a serpentine along the center line.

again, riding back in the opposite direction. Continue the pattern the length of the arena. All loops should be the same size, and when counting them, include the first and last loops, too. This type of serpentine can be ridden in all gaits: when riding it at the rising trot, you have to change the diagonal as you cross the centerline. Also, when riding the canter, change leads at the centerline (single or flying).

MOST COMMON MISTAKES
Single-Loop Serpentine **The Horse:** exhibits incorrect flexion and bend; goes against the rider's hand; is tight in the neck; is on the forehand. **The Rider:** doesn't ask for enough lateral bend; changes flexion and bend too early or too late; rides loops that are too shallow.

Double-Loop Serpentine See single-loop serpentine. **The Rider:** creates asymmetrical loops; plans the pattern poorly.

Serpentine Along the Centerline See single- and double-loop serpentine.

Serpentine Across the Arena See single- and double-loop serpentines, and serpentines along the centerline. **The Rider:** doesn't change diagonal when rising to the trot; changes canter leads too early or too late.

CORRECT AIDS The aids for these serpentines are basically identical since they all are merely a combination of turning (p. 1), and changing flexion and bend. In all, the horse must be flexed and bent toward the rider's inside leg.

In order to achieve this, initiate each serpentine with a half-halt on the outside
rein, while flexing the horse to the inside
with the inside rein. Your inside leg adds
pressure at the girth, and the outside leg
slides slightly behind the girth, thereby
controlling the haunches. Yield the outside rein slightly in order to enable the
outside neck muscles to stretch, but not
enough to allow the horse's outside
shoulder to "fall out."

In order to keep the loops symmetrical,
it's helpful to divide the arena length-
wise into four, evenly sized portions in
your mind. These quarterlines can be
used as reference points, making the
exercise easier.

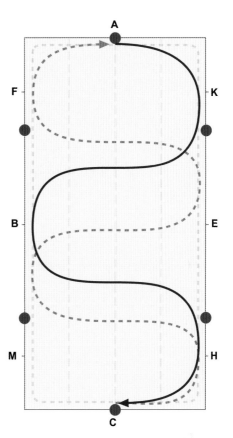

Serpentines across the arena
(three or four loops, respectively).

GOAL OF THE MOVEMENT All serpentines have a highly gymnastic effect on
the horse since they consist of meas-
ured, repetitive change in flexion and bend. The muscles on the
inside of the neck and trunk are shortened, and the outer ones
stretched—improving lateral bend. Also, through the alternation of
weight-bearing on the hind legs, the horse's flexibility is improved.
Serpentines are suitable for warming up the horse because the big,
bending lines can be ridden in all working gaits.

FAST FACTS Basic movements; can be ridden in the warm-up and
work phase of a schooling session; can be ridden in all basic gaits;
improve coordination and lateral mobility.

PYRAMID FACTOR Rhythm*, relaxation/suppleness***, contact**,
impulsion*, straightness**, collection*.

SHOULDER-IN
A forward-and-sideways (lateral) movement where the horse's forehand is led toward the center of the arena while being flexed and bent to the inside, with the haunches remaining on the track.

HOW IT'S SUPPOSED TO LOOK The shoulder-in—required at the trot, exclusively, in dressage tests—should be smooth and fluid, rhythmically secure, full of impulsion, with the horse always on the aids, and with the horse's front legs reaching and crossing over as much as possible. In the shoulder-in, the horse moves on three tracks so when facing him from the front and watching him move toward you, you can only see three of his legs.

During the shoulder-in, the horse is flexed to the inside and bent around the rider's inside leg, the hind legs move straight along the track.

MOST COMMON MISTAKES The Horse: exhibits little lateral bend; falls out through the outside shoulder; loses rhythm; is crooked; deviates from the line of travel; loses impulsion; hurries; labors; goes against the rider's hand; is tight in the neck; tilts his head at the poll. **The Rider:** begins the movement abruptly; asks for too little or too much flexion and bend; sits to the outside; takes her outside leg off the horse.

CORRECT AIDS Shoulder-in is commonly ridden on the track down the long side; however, it can also be ridden down the centerline or on any other straight line. To make the beginning of the movement easier, you can ride it out of a turn, and its best when coming out of the corner or after a volte. This way you can "carry" the flexion and bend from that movement into the shoulder-in.

For the shoulder-in, slightly shorten the inside rein, weight your inside seat bone slightly more, and determine the amount of flexion necessary with your inside hand. Your outside hand should yield accordingly, thereby allowing the horse the necessary stretch of the muscles on his outside, and also preventing him from tilting his head at the poll. However, the outside rein must not go too far forward, since this would allow the horse to fall out through his outside shoulder. This requires tact and sensitivity.

As soon as the horse is flexed appropriately, your inside hand must become "light" again in order not to block his inside hind leg but to instead allow it to step far underneath his center of gravity as he "steps into" the outside rein. Together with your seat and rein aids, you must slide your inside leg slightly behind the girth. This drives the horse forward-and-sideways and encourages him, in cooperation with your outside leg, to take on the necessary lateral bend.

Your outside leg must not be taken off the horse—as many riders do—but must continue to drive the horse's outside hind leg forward. After all, in the shoulder-in, this hind leg has more ground to cover. If you find your horse has difficulty with this, hold the whip in your outside hand to support your outside leg.

Supple

"Without the shoulder-in, nothing could happen! For me, a correct shoulder-in is part of the horse's basic training. When it's learned, I like to add the travers, which, especially when alternated with the leg-yield, is a great exercise for improving bend and collection. On the long side, I alternately ride a bit of travers, leg-yield, then travers again. When a horse is more trained, you can also ride the travers on a circle, especially decreasing and increasing its size: the horse moves in travers when decreasing it, and in shoulder-in when increasing it. A great exercise consists of riding in travers toward the centerline and in shoulder-in back to the track. Such exercises further suppleness and obedience. You can start to combine lateral gaits with a systematically trained horse from the end of his fifth, and beginning his sixth year. Remember, you must never merely ask for these movements without having a purpose in mind, or you will just tire out your horse."

JEAN BEMELMANS Riding master, trainer of the Spanish dressage team

Outside rein

All turns and lateral movements are ridden "on" the outside rein. The inside rein flexes the horse only, while the outside rein, in combination with the rider's legs, is important for the bend.

Complete the movement by releasing the inside flexion and bend, letting both legs slide back into their original position, and leading the horse's forehand back onto the track. As with the beginning of the movement, its completion should occur smoothly and without much hand influence.

GOAL OF THE MOVEMENT The shoulder-in is, like all lateral movements, a great exercise to improve the horse's "carrying power," and subsequently further collection since the respective hind leg is repeatedly asked to step more underneath the horse's center of gravity. At the same time, the horse is very effectively gymnasticized in his lateral trunk and neck muscles, since he has to shorten the muscles on the inside while stretching the muscles on the outside. The exercise also improves the mobility of the shoulder joints, and subsequently, free movement of the front legs out of the shoulders. Shoulder-in should always be practiced equally in both directions. It's popular to combine it with a transition into a travers (p. 145) or renvers (p. 111). It works the horse's entire body, and is a great exercise in coordination for the rider. For this reason, experienced trainers like to alternate between shoulder-in, travers, and renvers to prepare the horse for the piaffe (p. 95) and passage (p. 92). Lengthening the strides out of shoulder-in improves the forward-reaching tendency of the hind legs, and subsequently, impulsion.

FAST FACTS Advanced movement; can be ridden in the work phase of a schooling session; improves collection; improves lateral mobility and "carrying power"; helps rider gain self-control.

PYRAMID FACTOR Rhythm*, relaxation/suppleness*, contact*, impulsion***, straightness**, collection**.

SHOULDER-FORE

A preparatory forward-and-sideways (lateral) movement where the forehand is led toward the center of the arena yet is flexed and bent to the inside only slightly, while the haunches remain on the track.

HOW IT'S SUPPOSED TO LOOK The shoulder-fore is not required in dressage tests. It is a movement used purely for practice and training purposes. It should be smoothly and fluidly presented, rhythmically secure, full of impulsion, and the horse should be on the aids. Unlike shoulder-in (p. 126), the horse remains considerably straighter in the shoulder-fore, meaning *without* real longitudinal

A shoulder-fore (left) is ridden with clearly less lateral bend than shoulder-in (right).

bend. It is ridden with only a slight inside flexion and gentle bend through the rib cage. The horse's outside front leg and outside hind leg move on one track, the inside hind leg steps in the direction of the front legs, and between them (or their footprints, rather).

MOST COMMON MISTAKES The Horse: evades through his haunches; evades through his outside shoulder; exhibits inconsistent rhythm; is crooked; deviates from the line of travel; loses impulsion; hurries; labors; goes against the rider's hand; is tight in the neck; tilts his head at the poll. **The Rider:** initiates the movement too abruptly; asks for too much flexion and bend.

CORRECT AIDS Shoulder-fore can be ridden at any point of the arena—either down the entire long side, or beginning and ending at any place along it. Begin by first giving a half-halt, slightly shift your weight to your inside seat bone, and flex the horse a little with the inside rein (which you should have already shortened). Position your inside leg at the girth, creating a slight bend in the horse's rib cage and driving the horse's inside hind leg in the direction of—and between the footprints of—his front hooves. Keep your outside leg in a "guarding" position behind the girth, while your outside rein limits the amount of flexion inward.

If the horse doesn't take on the shoulder-fore position, but instead "runs through" his outside shoulder, it can help to temporarily ride (a few steps or strides) in counter-flexion. When the horse loses impulsion during the shoulder-fore, you should discontinue the exercise, and after riding a few strides straight ahead, begin again.

GOAL OF THE MOVEMENT Shoulder-fore improves the horse's coordination as well as his impulsion, "straightness," collection, and his willingness to "let through the aids." Also, problems in the poll (tilting), or when the horse has a tendency to evade through his outside shoulder, can be prevented or corrected by riding shoulder-fore. The canter, especially—both its straightness and quality—can be vastly improved.

FAST FACTS Progressive movement; degree of collection required; especially suitable for canter work; improves "carrying power."

PYRAMID FACTOR Rhythm*, relaxation/suppleness*, contact*, impulsion**, straightness***, collection**.

FLYING CHANGES IN SEQUENCE
A sequence of multiple flying changes where the horse changes lead every four, three, or two canter strides, or from a single canter stride to another.

HOW IT'S SUPPOSED TO LOOK Flying changes (p. 45) in a sequence, or "tempi changes in a series," should be straight, uphill, display good "jump," and have an even tempo and canter rhythm. They should be equal in ground cover and height. The rider must make sure to perform the changes divided equally on the required line, the same distance apart. If, for example, five, four-tempi changes are required across the entire diagonal, the third change should occur exactly on the centerline.

MOST COMMON MISTAKES The Horse: doesn't "jump through" each change evenly; is late behind in one or more changes; sways; does not travel a straight line; has a high croup; is tense; doesn't show enough of an "uphill" tendency; has "flat" or "shallow" changes; covers little ground; gets tight; falls on the forehand; has a tense back; fails to complete one or more required changes. **The Rider:** asks for the incorrect number of changes or strides; overuses aids; applies too obvious aids.

CORRECT AIDS Before you attempt to ride flying changes in a series, the individual change must already be confirmed—they should occur anytime at the rider's request in a relaxed manner without problems. Multiple tempi changes are nothing else but well-performed individual flying changes—with the only difference being they are ridden in succession.

You begin teaching the horse four-tempi changes. The one-tempi changes (from stride to stride) present the greatest degree of difficulty since they require advanced collection, a horse that's as straight as possible, and—in both rider and horse—a great amount of coordination. Four-, three-, and two-tempi changes are ridden quite similarly. For an inexperienced rider, keeping track of the number of changes and strides usually presents the biggest challenge! It's best to learn and acquire the feel for such difficult movements on a schoolmaster well-accustomed to the exercise.

Flying changes from "jump to jump"...

When teaching a horse tempi changes, it's best to begin on the long side of the arena, and initially only ask for two flying changes: from the "true" canter (p. 63) to counter-canter (p. 26) and back again. When this is achieved without tension or loss of concentration, you can slowly increase the number of changes, and then proceed to ask for some on the diagonal.

As an example, when you want to ride a series of changes across the diagonal, after turning (p. 1) off the short side at the canter, set your horse perfectly straight and get him "in front of you." To achieve this, apply a bit more forward-driving aids. After two or three canter strides (once you've completed "straightening" him) give the aid for the first flying change. For this, flex the horse minimally at the poll, while at the same time switching your leg positions: your outside leg slides forward toward the girth, while your inside leg slides behind the girth. The switching of the legs causes your hips to shift almost automatically into the new direction, thereby applying the necessary back and seat aid. The lead change that should (you hope!) follow this is counted as the first change, that is, number "One." The following canter strides, which must be kept collected and "uphill" by giving half-halts (p. 56), are counted as "Two," "Three," and "Four." At the end of the fourth canter stride, approximately, give the aid for the next change of lead—so the fifth canter stride is another flying change.

In order not to lose track of the number of changes you have ridden by the end of the diagonal, count the following way: "*One*, two, three, four; *two*, two, three, four; *three*, two, three, four," and so on. The same applies to three- and two-tempi changes. The rider who still has problems with counting or is always a whiff late with his aids, might consider counting aloud in the beginning.

...it's important the horse remains straight.

When the four-tempi changes turn out well, work your way up to the three-, and two-tempi changes accordingly. Only when these are solidly established, should you tackle the one-tempis. Here, it's best to initially try for only two, one-tempi changes—that is, "one-one." Then, ride a few normal canter strides again, and again ask for "one-one." When this works well, add a third one-tempi change: "one-one-one." With a talented and well-ridden horse, it often "clicks" after working on these mini-segments for some time—all of a sudden, four, five, or even more one-tempi changes can be achieved in a row. Setbacks along the way are normal, so try not to be concerned. Simply stay calm, reestablish relaxation and connection, and try again in a few days.

In the one-tempi changes, your aids should be reduced to a minimum in order to disturb the horse as little as possible in this highly collected movement that requires remarkable concentration, yet should still be sufficient enough to provide him with the support he needs. Ideally, the one-tempi changes should be ridden from a slight, barely visible rotation of your hips.

Not every horse (and not every rider) learns flying changes from stride to stride (one-tempis). For this reason, they should be reserved for experienced riders and horses with the athletic talent needed for this movement. Stubbornly practicing one-tempi changes when the horse is not ready or able can lead to tension, which could negatively affect all the other tempi change sequences he has achieved so far.

In all flying changes in sequence, you should make an effort to keep the horse as straight as possible and not change flexion back and forth unnecessarily. The straighter he remains through his body and neck, the easier it'll be. In fact, in one-tempi changes, you barely change flexion at all.

GOAL OF THE EXERCISE Bearing a special level of difficulty, flying changes are an excellent way of testing the quality of a rider's influence on the horse and his training, and how fine-tuned the communication is between horse and rider.

FAST FACTS Advanced movement; can be ridden in the work phase of a schooling session; level of difficulty increases from four-tempi to one-tempi changes; requires high level of coordination; required at Fourth Level (Advanced in the UK).

PYRAMID FACTOR Rhythm, relaxation/suppleness, contact, impulsion, straightness, collection.

EXTENDED WALK/TROT/CANTER

"Extended" refers to the most advanced stretching and lengthening of the horse's outline possible. The horse demonstrates maximum ground coverage, and in the trot and canter, an increased phase of suspension.

HOW IT'S SUPPOSED TO LOOK All "extended" gaits—regardless of whether ridden at walk, trot, or canter—are characterized by the horse covering more ground by exhibiting bigger movements, with the back muscles engaged. Extended *does not* mean simply going faster. The respective rhythm of the gait must be maintained: at the walk, this is four-beats; at the trot, two-beats; and at the canter, three-beats. With contact remaining even, the horse's frame lengthens for each stride.

Extended Walk The horse's forearm should reach out far from the shoulder—as much as its anatomical capacity allows—and his hind legs must also step farther forward, beyond the prints left by his front feet. Compared to the medium walk (p. 82), the stride is clearly longer. The extended walk should be engaged, with the legs stepping energetically. The horse will stretch slightly forward-and-downward toward the bit, and you must allow for the natural nodding motion of the head and neck with soft, following hands.

Extended Trot The horse—within the scope of his natural ability—should reach the greatest possible impulsion he can at the trot. The hind legs should "push" energetically and the amount of ground covered should increase accordingly. The hind hooves should step clearly beyond the prints of the front hooves.

In the extended walk, the horse should reach and step as far forward as possible.

Extended Canter The extended canter is characterized by demonstrating the greatest possible ground coverage with each individual canter stride. When compared, the difference from the medium canter must be clearly seen without the tempo changing or the horse moving "faster." The canter strides should be round and "uphill."

MOST COMMON MISTAKES

Extended Walk **The Horse:** exhibits inconsistent rhythm; paces; shows little engagement; is constricted; doesn't track-up; hurries; doesn't stretch his neck forward-and-downward; is tight in the neck; is above the bit; walks too similarly to medium walk.

Extended Trot **The Horse:** exhibits inconsistent rhythm; hurries; "runs"; is on the forehand; shows too little impulsion; is wide behind; is tense; has a tense back; demonstrates "toe-flicking" with his front legs; is tight in the neck; goes behind the vertical; goes against the rider's hand; breaks into the canter.

Extended Canter **The Horse:** exhibits "flat" strides; covers little ground; is on the forehand; is crooked; is on two tracks; rushes; is tight in the neck; goes behind the vertical; goes against the rider's hand.

CORRECT AIDS At all three basic gaits, the rider must ask the horse's hind legs to step ("swing") further forward underneath the horse's body. This means driving with your seat and leg aids is most important. However, you can't forget about the restraining rein aids, since they determine and preserve the desired frame.

Extended Walk As with all walk paces, you should first try to adjust to the horse's natural striding motion by "wiping" the saddle from back to front with your seat and pelvis in the rhythm of the walk. Note, however, that this should not turn into a "belly dance" of sorts but be done with a relatively quiet upper body. In order to achieve the increased forward "reach" of the front legs and overstep of the hind legs needed for the extended walk, this natural "forward-and-back" movement of your body should be slightly increased and combined with stronger leg aids. Your lower legs should deliver aids diagonally—that is, "crosswise." When, for example, the horse's right front leg steps forward, your left leg drives, and when the horse's left front leg steps forward, your right leg drives. This increased reach forward with the legs requires the horse to also stretch a bit longer in the neck,

When extending, the horse attains the largest amount of ground coverage possible at the trot.

which you must support by yielding with both reins: in order to maintain the contact, your hands must move backward and forward in the rhythm of the natural nodding motion of the horse's head and neck.

Extended Trot An optimal extended trot can only be acquired from good collection. This is because only then can the horse produce the necessary flexion in the haunches that is the prerequisite for converting an increase in "carrying power" (collection) into the ultimate "pushing power" (extension).

When you ask for an extension from the collected trot, you must bring the horse's hindquarters forward and "under" you. This can be done by using your back and applying brief leg pressure on both sides (you might want to give two or three leg aids in a row) as if you wanted to "compress a coiled spring" slightly more—and then again a little more. According to the law of conservation of energy (does this bring back dim memories from your school days?), energy that is built up this way is "waiting" to be released. And, when riding—in this case, when riding an extended trot—this release happens at the moment you slightly yield the reins, allowing the horse to let the built-up energy go "out the front door" by making his strides longer.

To keep control and avoid rhythm mistakes or the horse breaking into a canter, you must finely orchestrate your forward-driving, yielding, and restraining aids.

Extended Canter In order for this to be round, with an "uphill" canter stride, it should be established from a good, collected canter. In principle, the aids for extended canter are similar to those for the extended trot. The only differences are you drive and aid evenly on both sides at the trot, while at the canter, you put more weight on your inside seat bone, position your outside leg behind the girth, drive the horse forward with your inside leg, and slightly flex the horse in the poll to the inside with your inside hand.

"Catching" the impulsion

Riding an extended trot has nothing to do with "acceleration." In order to achieve the proper "expression," you must slightly "catch" the horse's forward impulsion, stride by stride.

Nonetheless, similar to riding an extended trot, you must build up energy before the canter extension. You have to "wake up" the hindquarters in preparation for the extension by giving half-halts and brief aids with your legs. Only at the moment when the "carrying" transfers into "pushing power," should you move your hands forward allowing the horse's neck to stretch forward as he extends his stride.

GOAL OF THE MOVEMENT All extended gaits are quite good indicators of the quality of the horse's training up to that point—they only turn out well when the horse is securely on the aids, aligned, with his back engaged (that is, when the requirements of the Training Pyramid have been met as training has progressed). Only then can the extended walk have more of a "striding" quality because the horse is able to round his back and step into your hand. Only then can the extended trot and canter be "lofty" and expressive because they stem from strengthened and active hindquarters, in combination with a swinging back.

A special bonus of integrating periods of extended canter into your training regimen is that it helps preserve the horse's joy of movement.

FAST FACTS Advanced movement; can be ridden in the work phase of a schooling session; required at Third Level (Medium/Advanced Medium in the UK) and upward; requires (and improves) "pushing power."

PYRAMID FACTOR Rhythm, relaxation/suppleness*, contact, impulsion**, straightness, collection*.

Never ask for too much

In the extended gaits, whether at walk, trot or canter, the rider should not ask for too much, but accept his horse's limitations. This especially applies to the extended trot, where asking (wrongly) for "a faster rhythm" can cause the horse to "flick up" his front toes in order to comply. With such a horse, less is often more—and paramount are his even rhythm and engaged back. The same is true for walk and canter. When a horse is at a physical disadvantage, you can make his extensions look better to the judges by clearly differentiating them from the paces you ride before and afterward.

The extended canter—as shown in the picture—should cover as much ground as possible and with an "uphill" tendency.

FLEXION
A lateral turning of the horse's head with the poll being the pivot point.

HOW IT'S SUPPOSED TO LOOK Flexion—like bend and lateral bend (p. 76)—is neither a movement nor an exercise. However, it's such a basic "ingredient" in riding and a prerequisite for so many movements and exercises that I'd like to explain it.

The flexion I am concerned with occurs mainly in the poll. While the bringing of the horse's chin toward the underside of his neck is considered a type of flexion, it is *lateral flexion* that I discuss here. This is the side-to-side flexion at the poll that brings the horse's cheek toward one side of the neck or the other. From there it proceeds very slightly down through the horse's neck. When flexed one way or the other, the horse's ears must remain at the same level.

Many riders make the mistake of overflexing their horse, constantly pulling on the inside rein. All they achieve is a horse that leans on the inside rein, falls out through the outside shoulder, and fails to step underneath his center of gravity and round his back. Hence, overflexion does much more harm than good! The horse should be flexed only as much he gives at the poll so you can see the corner of his inside eye (see riding in position, p. 142).

MOST COMMON MISTAKES The Horse: falls out through the outside shoulder; goes against the rider's hand; is tight in the neck; flexes at the base of the neck instead of the poll. **The Rider:** overflexes the horse; "pulls" the horse's head around.

CORRECT AIDS In order to achieve flexion, you mostly use your rein aids. In general, preparation for any dressage movement requires inside flexion. First you slightly shorten your inside rein, then turn your wrist to the inside with your thumb at the top. With a horse that is very "rideable" and "on the aids," this rotation of your wrist should be sufficient, but with a less well-schooled horse, you may initially require more intensive aids. If need be, you might even have to move your entire hand slightly backward or sideways. However, you must immediately follow this by yielding your hand in order to prevent the horse from leaning on the inside rein.

GOAL OF THE MOVEMENT Flexion can be used to test how easily a horse yields at the poll. Furthermore, as mentioned, it is prerequisite for most dressage movements and exercises, starting with the simplest ones, like turning (p. 1), to the initiation of a far more difficult canter pirouette (p. 99). In the majority of cases, flexion is required in combination with bend—that is, lateral bend. Only when a horse is correctly flexed and bent is he able to execute turns without damaging his joints.

FAST FACTS Prerequisite for many movements; improves lateral mobility of the poll and neck muscles; necessary for keeping a horse sound.

PYRAMID FACTOR Rhythm, relaxation/suppleness*, contact**,
impulsion, straightness*, collection.

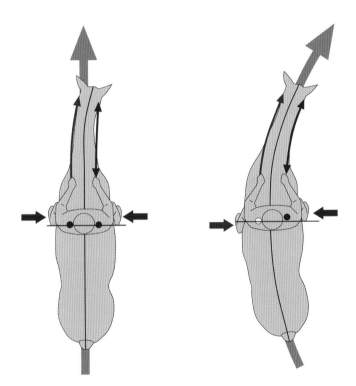

The difference between flexion and
bend. The horse on the left is
flexed, and the horse on the right is
flexed and bent (lateral bend).

COMPLEMENTARY EXERCISE

"RIDING IN POSITION"

Flex the horse's head and neck for several strides while also asking for a slight bend through the rib cage. A preliminary exercise for forward-and-sideways (lateral) movements later on in training.

HOW IT'S SUPPOSED TO LOOK When "riding in position" you must make sure that the horse yields in the throatlatch, and not at the base of the neck. The horse's body should remain aligned, which means his neck does not bend sideways in an exaggerated manner.

The horse should move in the correct, steady rhythm with an even tempo for the respective basic gait. He yields at the poll, bends his neck a little, becomes lighter on the inside rein, and steps more into the outside rein. The inside front and hind legs remain on one track, while the outside hind leg moves slightly inside the track made by the outside front leg.

MOST COMMON MISTAKES The Horse: is tense in the poll; leans on the inside rein; bends at the base of his neck, rather than the top of his neck near the throatlatch; tilts his head at the poll. **The Rider:** overflexes the horse.

CORRECT AIDS In order to "ride in position," slightly shorten the inside rein. Then rotate your hand to the inside just a bit, allowing the outside rein to go forward slightly. The horse should respond by turning his head to the side, starting at the poll. His outside neck muscles should clearly "bulge" and become visible, while the inside ones appear to become "flatter." When changing flexion, the look of the neck muscles should be reversed: the previously pronounced side becomes flat, and the other more clearly visible. When flexing a horse in order to turn (p. 1), this pronunciation of neck musculature is only brief.

For gymnastic purposes, you can "ride in position" for several strides. However, you must be sure not to flex too much—do not "pull the horse's head around" as this blocks the horse's inside hind leg from coming forward and under him, and in the long run, creates more tightness and tension than stretching and suppleness.

You can also combine "riding in position" with bending. Together, flexion and bend result in lateral bend (p. 76), which simply means adjusting a horse from poll to tail evenly on a curved line (a circle or volte, for example). If you are "riding in position" when already bent to a loop, curve, or arc, ask for slightly more flexion than normal, for as long as necessary until the horse yields in the poll. At the moment the horse "gives" to the flexion, the rider must immediately soften his inside hand, "rewarding" the horse. Avoid constantly "plucking" on the inside rein to the rhythm of the movement—this doesn't make the poll more supple; it deadens the horse's mouth.

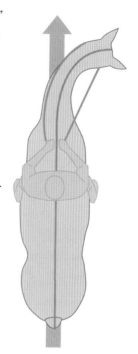

It's incorrect to pull the horse's neck sideways–that is, to over-flex it like this.

GOAL OF THE MOVEMENT "Riding in position" is a gymnasticizing exercise. It helps to further the ability of the poll and neck near the throatlatch to yield—prerequisites for successfully riding other movements. It also improves a horse's lateral bend and his ability to bring his outside hind leg forward, under, and slightly inside his outside front leg.

FAST FACTS Basic exercise; can be ridden at all working and collected paces; improves lateral mobility of the poll and the neck muscles.

PYRAMID FACTOR Rhythm*, relaxation/suppleness**, contact**, impulsion*, straightness***, collection*.

In the travers, the horse
moves in lateral bend on
four tracks.

TRAVERS (HAUNCHES-IN)

A forward-and-sideways (lateral) movement where the horse looks toward and is bent in the direction of travel, with his forehand on the track and his hindquarters placed toward the center of the arena.

HOW IT'S SUPPOSED TO LOOK The travers should be ridden forward smoothly and with impulsion. The horse's front legs and hind legs cross over each other as much as possible, and he moves on four tracks. Here's an example to make it clearer: when on the left rein, with the horse flexed and bent to the left, his front legs travel the long side of the arena—on two tracks—while his hindquarters travel on two separate tracks to the inside at a 30-degree angle from the rail.

The travers can be ridden on any line, not only along the fence or wall. You complete the travers similarly to completing a volte (p. 171), by riding back onto the track. Travers can be ridden at walk, trot, and canter, though when in the latter, it's mainly at a collected pace with occasional lengthenings to a working pace to prevent loss of impulsion. Generally, you should avoid riding travers at the canter since it can aggravate some horses' inclination to shift the hindquarters to the inside.

MOST COMMON MISTAKES The Horse: isn't forward enough; hurries; loses impulsion; loses rhythm; deviates from the line of travel; is tight in the neck; goes against the rider's hand; tilts his head at the poll. **The Rider:** asks for too little or too much flexion; pushes the horse too far sideways and not enough forward; shifts weight incorrectly (sits to the outside).

CORRECT AIDS Travers can be started at any given point on a track, though most commonly it is begun just after passing through a corner. This gives you the advantage of "carrying" the corner's existing flexion and bend into the travers. Keep the flexion and bend until the first letter at the beginning of the long side of the arena, put more

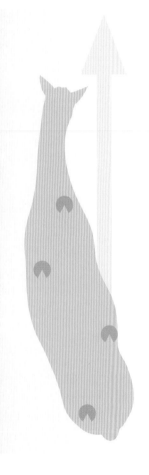

The travers viewed from above: the forehand remains on the track, while the haunches move inward.

weight on your inside seat bone, thereby positioning the outside leg behind the girth and driving the haunches sideways toward the center of the arena. Your inside leg—which the horse bends around—should be at the girth, driving him forward. Your inside hand maintains the horse's flexion, while your outside hand "gives" forward as necessary to allow the neck and trunk muscles on the outside to stretch. At the same time, however, your outside hand must keep enough contact to prevent the horse from falling out through his outside shoulder.

When you begin the travers on a straight line rather than from a corner, your inside hand, inside driving leg, and outside leg (in a "guarding" position) all become active simultaneously. At the end of the travers, your outside leg slides back into its original position, and together with your inside leg, now drives the horse forward as his hindquarters leave the inside parallel tracks they were on and return to the track along the rail, aligned with the forehand.

GOAL OF THE MOVEMENT Like all lateral movements, the travers improves the horse's sensitivity to the rider's leg aids. Furthermore, it gymnasticizes the horse through his longitudinal axis (lateral bending of the body), improves lateral mobility of shoulders and hip joints, and the weight-carrying ability of the haunches, especially when you alternate between the travers and the shoulder-in (p. 126). Travers is also a popular preparatory exercise for the half-pass (p. 148).

FAST FACTS Advanced movement; improves collection; suitable for the work phase of a schooling session; teaches lateral mobility and "carrying power."

PYRAMID FACTOR Rhythm, relaxation/suppleness*, contact*, impulsion**, straightness**, collection***.

In the half-pass, the horse's legs should reach far across each other.

HALF-PASS

A forward-and-sideways (lateral) movement along an imaginary diagonal line, where the horse—flexed and bent in direction of travel with his body parallel to the long side of the arena—moves with his forehand slightly ahead of his haunches, and his outside legs crossing over his inside legs.

HOW IT'S SUPPOSED TO LOOK A half-pass looks like a travers—the only difference is that the horse doesn't move along a track but away from it at an angle. Half-passes can be ridden along the diagonal from long side to long side, across half the width of the arena (from or to the centerline), along the diagonal and back again, and as a zigzag (p. 175).

The half-pass along the diagonal goes from one long side of the arena to the opposite long side; the half-pass across half the width of the arena only from the centerline to the track or from the track to the centerline. Half-passes along the diagonal and back again only go half the width of the arena (to the centerline) but lead back to the track you began on. In zigzag half-passes, you change direction after a specified number of meters or strides. The steeper the angle of the half-pass—the more sideways it is ridden—the more lateral bend is necessary, which is correspondingly more difficult.

Half-passes can be ridden at the walk, trot, and canter, though in the latter mainly at a collected pace. In order to prevent loss of impulsion, you can temporarily increase the pace to a working canter and then bring it back again.

All half-passes should appear smooth, even, full of impulsion, and "flow" forward, with the horse's front legs and hind legs reaching out sideways and crossing as much as possible. The horse is flexed to the inside and bent around your inside leg. His body is always parallel to the long side of the arena, with the forehand slightly leading the

"Rating" the level of work

Travers and especially half-passes should not be ridden too early, or too frequently, in a horse's training. Lateral stress put on the legs, which increases as the work level increases, requires you to introduce these exercises cautiously. Younger horses, especially, are very susceptible to injury. The higher the degree of collection, the less the stress: a rider who doesn't take all this into account risks sinew, ligament, and cartilage damage.

The half-pass at the trot.

A half-pass to the left showing ideal lateral freedom of the shoulder.

hindquarters. A half-pass is only completed when the horse's forehand and hindquarters are realigned again on the track.

MOST COMMON MISTAKES The Horse: is not parallel to the long side; leads with his hindquarters; shows little (hardly any) lateral bend; loses rhythm; loses impulsion; isn't smooth through the movement; "runs"; loses cadence; hesitates; is on the forehand; is tight in the neck; tilts his head at the poll; goes against the rider's hand. **The Rider:** drives the horse too much sideways and too little forward; flexes and bends the horse incorrectly; doesn't ride the movement from letter to letter; shifts her weight incorrectly (sits to the outside).

CORRECT AIDS In order to begin a half-pass correctly—regardless whether you begin at the rail or the centerline—it's important to allow the forehand to lead immediately, as this prevents the common mistakes of the haunches leading. For this reason, it can be helpful to begin each half-pass by "thinking" shoulder-in (p. 126) or shoulder-fore (p. 129). First flex the horse in the direction of travel and ride in a shoulder-in-like manner for a stride, before sliding your outside leg further behind the girth, shifting your weight onto the inside seat bone, and driving the horse *forward* with the inside leg at the girth, and *sideways* with the outside leg. You have successfully initiated the movement when the horse's inside front leg moves forward-and-sideways in the direction of travel first, with the "rest" of the horse following this leg. Allow your inside rein to maintain this flexion, yielding the outside rein slightly so the outside of the horse's neck and trunk muscles can stretch. As soon as the horse has taken on the appropriate flexion, your inside hand must become soft again (give the rein forward), so as not to block the forward-striding motion of the corresponding shoulder and hind leg.

In addition, I recommend thinking of the shoulder-in whenever changing direction within a half-pass in order to prevent mistakes and perform it in fluidly. You do this by very briefly setting the horse straight, then riding into the new direction of travel in a shoulder-in-like manner for a moment, before your sideways-driving leg collects the haunches again. During this brief moment of straightening as you prepare to change flexion and bend, you must switch aids: adjust your seat to the new direction of travel—that is, weight the opposite seat bone more—move the inside leg behind the girth, make the outside leg the new inside leg, and "swap" the rein aids.

The movement is completed by maintaining flexion, bend, and sideways-driving aids until the "entire" horse—that is, his haunches,

The half-pass as a gymnastic exercise

"For me, a half-pass is an excellent gymnasticizing tool. It allows you to work on lateral bend—which, at the same time, is also a prerequisite to achieving smooth half-passes going in both directions. The half-pass is also a movement for teaching the horse to step really well into the outside rein.

"To prepare the horse, I first ride the combination 'shoulder-in-volte-shoulder-in.' If this works well, I begin half-passes. At first, they should be ridden at a very shallow angle in order to maintain rhythm and impulsion. Only when the horse can execute solid and fluid half-passes at this angle, should you tackle steeper ones. Whenever you face a problem or setback, you must immediately ride the half-pass at the shallower angle again. Only then can the horse maintain his impulsion in steeper angled half-passes, expressively reaching out sideways with his legs. I seldom train steep half-passes, such as those required at Grand Prix level, except one or two days before a test.

"In general, you should not over-practice individual movements. In daily training—depending on the horse—two to five half-passes on each rein should be plenty, though during the learning phase, perhaps a few more. When your preparation is rather too ambitious, movements will suffer and deteriorate as a result."

HUBERTUS SCHMIDT
Team Olympic medalist, five-time German Champion

too—is back on the track. Only then can you straighten the horse again and ride forward.

Only experienced riders are able to deal with the accumulation of aids needed to change direction within a half-pass, since orchestrating them all requires a great amount of coordination and a lot of "feel" for movement. For this reason, zigzag half-passes, which consist of frequent changes of direction from right to left and vice versa, are only required in higher level dressage tests. When performed at the canter with flying changes at each change of direction, zigzags are found at Intermediaire II and above.

Half-passes along the diagonal or along the diagonal and back to the track are not required before Third Level (Medium/Advanced Medium in the UK).

GOAL OF THE MOVEMENT Half-passes gymnasticize the horse through his body (his longitudinal axis); further the lateral mobility of the shoulders and hip joints; and improve the "carrying power" of his haunches. A half-pass is both a collected as well as a "collecting" movement, meaning it schools and improves the ability of the horse to be in self-carriage. Furthermore, it exposes the quality of the rider's influence since any seat and/or aid mistakes are sure to be reflected.

FAST FACTS Advanced to very advanced movement; required from Third Level (Medium/Advanced Medium in the UK) onward; ridden in the work phase of a schooling session; improves lateral mobility and "carrying power."

PYRAMID FACTOR Rhythm, relaxation/suppleness*, contact, impulsion**, straightness**, collection***.

LENGTHENING STRIDE

At the trot or the canter, increasing the pace (from work-ing to medium) whereby each stride covers more ground.

HOW IT'S SUPPOSED TO LOOK In a correct lengthening of stride, the horse maintains the same rhythm and tempo (the rate of repetition of the rhythm) of the trot or canter, and elongates both his stride and his body frame. Depending on a horse's level of training and balance, the amount of lengthening will vary, as well as the elongation of his frame. Lengthenings, required only in lower level dressage tests, resemble the medium trot and canter (pp. 85 and 89). The difference is, a lengthened trot, for example, is developed from the working gait, while a medium trot is performed from a collected trot—the horse's balance and center of gravity are in a different place as a result of his more advanced level of training. For this reason, lengthening stride is an appropriate preliminary step, for both horse and rider, in preparation for later medium pace requirements.

MOST COMMON MISTAKES The Horse: hurries; "runs"; exhibits inconsistent rhythm; is on the forehand; is tight in the neck; goes behind the vertical; demonstrates little thrust from the hindquarters; doesn't lengthen enough or at all; breaks into the canter. **The Rider:** uses too much hand; doesn't sufficiently prepare by driving the horse forward and "gathering" the hind legs under the horse's body; is crooked; has a busy seat; aids incorrectly.

When lengthening the stride, rhythm has priority.

CORRECT AIDS The aids for lengthening stride are basically the same as for asking for the medium trot or canter, only the result (the lengthening itself) is less pronounced in terms of expression and development of impulsion.

Before lengthening stride, which is either ridden on the diagonal or down the long side of the arena, get the horse's attention with a few half-halts and drive the haunches more underneath the horse's body mass ("activate" the hind legs) using your back and leg pressure at the girth. It is helpful to use the corner before the diagonal or long side for this purpose: as you ride through the corner, it is easier to ask the horse to bring the haunches under his body and "gather" him prior to lengthening stride.

As soon as the horse is completely straight after the corner, lengthen his stride by moving your hands forward while increasing your driving aids. If you prepare sufficiently, as I've outlined, the lengthening will usually occur. Problems that do arise are almost always caused by the rider.

GOAL OF THE MOVEMENT As said before, lengthening stride prepares for the medium paces later on when the horse's training has advanced and he is ridden in collection. It's used with young horses to learn to extend their working gaits, since it doesn't require as much strength and balance. In the course of training, lengthening stride, in combination with shortening stride, provides a great opportunity to systematically gymnasticize the horse in daily training. It also maintains his desire to "go forward," as well as improving his general "letting through of the aids."

FAST FACTS Basic exercise; ridden at the end of the warm-up and in the work phase of a schooling session; creates "pushing power"; revives impulsion; motivates the horse to go forward; required in lower level dressage tests.

PYRAMID FACTOR Rhythm**, relaxation/suppleness**, contact**, impulsion*, straightness, collection.

TRANSITION
Changing from one gait into the next, as well as changing pace within a gait.

HOW IT'S SUPPOSED TO LOOK Transitions—including half-halts (p. 56) and full halts (p. 49)—should be ridden fluidly and smoothly without a lot of obvious effort from the rider. The aids should be almost invisible. The horse should remain evenly on the aids, stretch a bit more toward the rider's hand, and always keep his poll the highest point. A transition should always feel as if it's happening from "back to front," completely free of restraint.

When performing transitions from gait to gait, or *within* a gait, such as a lengthening (from a working gait—p. 15) or an extension (from a collected gait—p. 165), or when shortening stride and returning to a collected state, the hindquarters (the "engine") must initially provide impulsion, and then just as easily be able to "absorb" it again. Only when your horse is capable of this can you be sure that your transitions will be smooth and without hesitation.

When planning a transition, give a half-halt to encourage the horse's hindquarters to take up more weight so he is prepared for the new gait.

MOST COMMON MISTAKES The Horse: hesitates; goes against the rider's hand; is tight in the neck; doesn't "let the aids through"; transitions late or early; doesn't clearly change gait or pace; is on the forehand; exhibits inconsistent rhythm; trails his hindquarters; takes up little or no weight with his haunches.

CORRECT AIDS Transitions are essential when training horses. The rider who masters them is on the right track. In terms of which aids you need when, you must consider the different types of transitions there

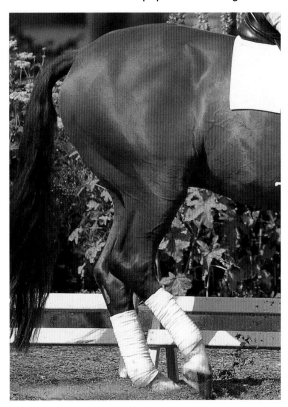

are: is it a) an increase in pace within a gait (p. 185); b) a reduction in pace within a gait; c) a transition into a gait; d) a transition out of a gait; or e) a transition between two movements (for example, piaffe—p. 95—to passage—p. 92).

All transitions require perfect orchestration of forward-driving and restraining aids. If you want to lengthen or extend the stride (a)—that is, increase the pace—you must prepare by bringing the hindquarters further underneath the horse's center of gravity with your seat and leg aids (as described in lengthening stride—p. 153—and medium trot and canter—pp. 85 and 89), and then "open the door" and release the horse's built-up forward energy by giving with the reins. So, the forward-driving aids are, in combination with a yielding hand, more important when lengthening or extending the stride.

Downward transition within a gait: the horse is "gathered" (left) and his frame "closes up" and the stride is "shortened" (right).

When reducing the stride (b)—that is, "gathering" the horse to decrease the pace—it's the opposite. You must continue to drive with both legs in order keep the horse's hind legs active, enabling him to

take up more weight with his haunches. Simultaneously, give stronger restraining rein aids, which shorten the horse's frame (also leading to additional lowering of the haunches). Note however, your rein aids must *not* end up "pulling" on the horse incessantly, since that would block the horse's back, hindering, if not preventing, the horse from taking up the necessary weight behind. This orchestration of forward-driving and restraining aids is called a half-halt (p. 56).

Half-halts are also applied in the next type of transition: changing from one gait to another. When you want to move upward from a slower gait to a faster gait (c), apply a half-halt to get the horse's attention. Then, give the aids for either the trot (p. 10) or the canter (p. 5). The horse's response should be immediate—he should not take any intermediate or unsure steps or strides.

Transitions from a faster gait to a slower gait (d) should also happen spontaneously. Here I'll describe three possibilities: trot-to-walk, canter-to-trot, and canter-to-walk.

All transitions should be ridden smoothly without a lot of effort on the rider's part—that is, with aids invisible to an observer.

Trot-to-Walk Slightly shorten both reins by briefly turning your fists slightly inward. At the same time, drive the horse's hind legs further underneath his center of gravity with your lower legs (use light, momentary pressure from the calves). Apply your (almost invisible) rein and leg aids in quick succession until the horse has accepted the half-halt and transitions down to the walk. At the moment he changes gait, your hands must slide smoothly forward to allow him to stretch his neck, give him freedom to reach forward with his shoulders, and encourage him to stride under with his hind legs. Depending on the pace of the walk, your rein length may need to be adjusted. Using your seat and legs, continue to drive the horse into your hand in the rhythm of the walk.

Canter-to-Trot This transition is best achieved by simply ceasing your canter aids: slide your outside leg forward, release the slight inside flexion, and weight both seat bones evenly again. Most horses will

Extra notes

Transitions are so essential in working a horse correctly that they are judged individually in dressage tests. There are separate marks for transitions before and after the extensions. This separate evaluation continues through Grand Prix, where the transitions into piaffe and passage play a substantial role in the overall score. With about 36 individual movements in the test, six marks reflect the transitions between piaffe and passage: from passage into piaffe; from piaffe into passage; from trot into passage; from passage into the trot or canter.

transition into the trot almost automatically. However, you must prevent the horse from falling on his forehand, so exactly at the moment when the horse transitions into the trot, increase your driving aids again into your restraining—then slightly yielding—hand, using your back and legs (half-halt). This makes sure that the hind legs stride forward underneath the horse's body, which allows his forehand to slightly "rise up." When the horse doesn't respond to the aids for a downward transition into the trot but just continues to canter, it often helps to briefly flex him to the outside.

Canter-to-Walk A canter-to-walk transition with a horse that's well collected and cantering "roundly" uphill is—most of the time—easier than with horse that's green or strung-out. In either case, to achieve a successful canter-to-walk transition, you must first "internalize" the rhythm of the canter—that is, the three distinct beats. This way, over time, you can develop some feel for the moment of suspension—the instant when all the horse's legs are briefly in the air at the same time. Ideally, you should apply the aids for the downward transition at the beginning of this suspension phase. At that moment, the horse's hind legs are about to reach far underneath his center of gravity and the horse moves distinctly "uphill." This "uphill" tendency is maintained through the following phases of the canter before the nature of the gait angles the horse's forehand more toward the ground. When the aid to walk is given at the right moment, the transition will successfully occur with the desired "uphill" tendency. If, on the other hand, you give the aid at the wrong moment (during a phase *prior to* the moment of suspension), the horse can't help but fall on his forehand!

To give the aid for the downward transition from the canter to the walk, slide your outside leg forward while releasing the slight inside flexion, drive the horse more toward your hand with both legs, and increase your restraining rein aids. At the very moment the horse senses the half-halt and changes from the three-beat rhythm of the canter into the four-beat rhythm of the walk, yield your hands, and if necessary, let the reins become slightly longer to allow the horse to stretch his neck. Only this way can the horse's back "round" at the moment of half-halting, making it possible for a rhythmically secure transition, followed by a rhythmically pure walk.

The most difficult transitions are between piaffe and passage. They require maximum strength, coordination, and "throughness" on the part of the horse, as well as a great deal of rider "feel" and coordination. For this reason, they are not required before Intermediaire II. Like other transitions, those from passage-to-piaffe and from piaffe-to-passage should be fluid, and free of constraint and rhythm mistakes. The amount of strength the horse needs is enormous since you change from a trot-like movement with an extremely short phase of suspension (piaffe) into a trot movement with a suspension phase extended to the maximum (passage) or vice versa. These transitions are only successful when the horse has learned both the piaffe and the passage correctly in the first place.

Passage-to-Piaffe When in the passage, approaching the point where you want to execute a piaffe, you must begin to slightly increase your restraining rein aids, while at the same time shifting your weight slightly forward and driving the horse with both legs (equilaterally and simultaneously) toward the fixed (yet slightly "breathing") hand. The combination of these aids "breaks up" and stops the suspension of the passage. The horse's hindquarters lower even further, allowing him to transition to "lifting up" and putting down his front and hind feet rhythmically, almost on the spot.

Piaffe-to-Passage For most horses this transition is even more difficult, since they have to turn the extreme "carrying power" of the up-and-down motion of the hind legs in piaffe into an upward-and-*forward* motion that propels their entire weight (and that of the rider, too) into the long phase of suspension desired in passage. With correct aids you can support your horse in this; however, your role is also very difficult!

When transitioning from piaffe (photos 1 and 2) into passage (photo 3), the horse must convert his "uphill" movement into a "forward-uphill" movement.

First of all, you must alert the horse that he will soon have to "exit" the piaffe and change into the passage. You do this by driving him increasingly forward while at the same time restraining with the reins, then "give" with both reins slightly forward at the right moment, in order to "release" the horse's contained movement. Lighten your seat and give slightly stronger, forward-driving aids with your calves—an aid combination that enables the horse to propel forward-and-upward from the hindquarters while continuing to round his back. To avoid the horse simply breaking into a trot rather than passage, you have to "gather" the horse with the reins again while continuing to drive with a light (*not* squeezing!) leg.

A small tip: don't get frantic during this transition. Allow yourself and your horse time to find the new rhythm. Think less about "riding out of the piaffe" and more about "releasing the passage." Then, the transition will most likely be more relaxed.

GOAL OF THE MOVEMENT Transitions are the "knee bends" of horse training. They are pure muscle training, regardless of the form

they take, though they mainly work the muscles of the hindquarters and the back. This is because in all types of transitions, the rider asks the horse to increase the flexion in the haunches—that is, to increase the angles of the joints in the hindquarters. At the moment they are flexed, the "carrying" muscles of the hind legs are in action—building and strengthening them for the long run.

Furthermore, when you ride transitions, many aids—provided they are correctly applied—come together to round the horse's back, thereby strengthening it. This, in combination with the steadily growing strength of the hindquarters, also improves the horse's ability to "let through the aids." For this reason, transitions can be called the "nuts and bolts" of riding in general.

FAST FACTS Exercise can span from easy to very difficult; schools both "carrying" and "pushing power."

PYRAMID FACTOR Rhythm*, relaxation/suppleness**, contact***, impulsion***, straightness*, collection***.

RELEASE

A brief release of contact where the rider extends one or both hands forward along the crest of the horse's neck for a few strides.

HOW IT'S SUPPOSED TO LOOK When you "release" the reins, you extend one or both hands forward in the direction of the horse's mouth, to the point where your arm(s) are almost stretched right out so the reins go forward along the horse's crest. The horse may elongate his frame a bit forward-and-downward; however, ideally he maintains the same carriage, balance, pace, and tempo, and remains on the aids. Theoretically, a release can be ridden in all basic gaits, but it's commonly asked for at the trot and canter.

MOST COMMON MISTAKES The Horse: goes against the rider's hand; tosses his head; falls onto the forehand; loses contact. **The Rider:** doesn't demonstrate enough of a release; doesn't release at all; doesn't release for long enough; holds her hands too high.

During the release of reins, the horse should remain on the aids.

CORRECT AIDS Releasing the reins is an exercise, and you do not "give aids" for it, as such. However, you can practice a correct release. Just before the release, it's best to position the horse's poll a bit deeper for a brief moment with a tiny left-right movement of the hands while simultaneously driving the horse forward with your seat and legs. This way you have already indicated to the horse the direction you want him to keep stretching his neck. The release should not be done jerkily, since the horse might be startled by a sudden forward movement from your hands. It's better to let them go forward slowly and smoothly in one movement, and bring them back into their original position the same way.

GOAL OF THE MOVEMENT In the course of a dressage test, a release gives the judges a great opportunity to evaluate contact, relaxation and suppleness, and obedience. The horse should willingly stay in light contact and on the aids. If there are hidden issues in these areas, they will usually become apparent at this time. You can see it particularly with horses that are "clamped" between hand and bit by physically strong riders—they will resist this harsh hand influence at the moment of release.

Releasing the reins in daily training is a great exercise for you to find out for yourself the true state of contact, relaxation and suppleness, and obedience. This check can be done briefly, too—you don't have to release the reins over stretches of several strides, except in dressage tests. It's sufficient to just move one or both hands forward slightly more than normal once in a while for one or two trot or canter strides. If the horse responds by getting quicker, running, or tossing his head, you need to reevaluate your training program.

FAST FACTS Basic exercise; can be performed (and should be possible) at any time.

PYRAMID FACTOR Rhythm*, relaxation/suppleness**, contact*, impulsion**, straightness, collection.

The collected trot.

COLLECTION

The product of increased engagement from lowering of the hindquarters and the resulting lighter forehand. When a horse is collected, his outline appears shorter from poll to tail, and the length of his strides or steps are shorter, too.

HOW IT'S SUPPOSED TO LOOK Whether you collect the horse at the walk, trot, or canter, a collected gait should always be rhythmically pure and appear "lofty." This loftiness of stride, or elevation, is the result of the horse taking up more weight behind and allowing his forehand to "rise." When the raising of the neck and forehand and the lowering of the haunches are directly connected as they should be, you have achieved the desired state of *relative elevation*. When the horse's head and neck is physically "pulled" upward but his haunches remain as usual (not lowered and flexed accordingly), it is called *absolute elevation*—this is not collection, but an undesired and faulty physical state.

Depending on the gait, the state of collection appears slightly different:

Collected Walk In the collected walk, the steps cover less ground, and the hind feet track *behind* the prints of the front feet. Every single leg should be markedly lifted and set down; the pace marching and vigorous; the horse's body and neck slightly compressed; the poll the highest point; and the nose approaching the vertical.

When collected, the horse becomes more lofty and expressive in his way of going.

Collected Trot Unlike the walk, the trot and canter have a moment of suspension, where all four legs are airborne. In the trot, this is when the horse switches the diagonal leg pairs. Besides shortening the length of stride (the hind feet step just *into* the prints of the front feet) and the compression of the body and lowering of the hindquarters, collection at the trot is characterized especially by a longer phase of suspension—the horse remains airborne longer. It's most pronounced in horses at and beyond Fourth Level (Advanced in the UK).

Building strength systematically

"When training, you should cater to a horse's strengths. Of course, you must also work on his weaknesses, however, not to any great extent. Unfortunately, many riders don't take enough time to slowly develop movements through gymnastic work, and build a horse's strength systematically. Instead, they ask the horse to continuously perform the same movement, and the result is it just gets worse and worse. Instead of riding countless pirouettes, for example, you should improve the horse's ability to carry his weight behind through work in collection. Then, the pirouettes will automatically become better. Walk-canter transitions in brief succession are always important since they further the building up of strength and the 'letting through of the aids.' When doing these, I prefer transitions from true canter to walk and back to true canter."

HOLGER SCHMEZER
German dressage coach

Collected Canter The collected canter is also characterized by a longer phase of suspension, loftier strides, and a shortened frame. The longer the phase of suspension, the more time the horse has to come far underneath his center of gravity before touching the ground with the first hind leg. At the collected canter, the horse—through his frame, stride, suspension, and "uphill" tendency—should look as if he is cantering quietly up a mountain.

MOST COMMON MISTAKES

Collected Walk The Horse: exhibits inconsistent rhythm; ambles; paces; jigs; shows little or no expression; shows little engagement; just slows down; drags his feet; doesn't lift feet markedly; goes behind the vertical; doesn't step into the rider's hand; exhibits little collection; hesitates.

Collected Trot The Horse: shows little or no expression; just slows down; has no impulsion; is tight in the neck; is on the forehand; goes behind the vertical; is in absolute elevation; is above the bit; exhibits inconsistent rhythm; shows little collection; has a tense back; swishes his tail; strides tensely; "hovers."

Collected Canter The Horse: exhibits inconsistent rhythm; "four-beats"; is tight in the neck; goes behind the vertical; is in absolute elevation; has a tense back; shows little collection; doesn't show enough flexion in his hindquarters (doesn't "sit down" enough); drags his feet; isn't showing an "uphill" tendency; hurries through the sequence of strides; shows little suspension.

CORRECT AIDS There are really no special aids for collecting a horse. Rather, the aids you normally give for the working trot and canter, and medium walk, are used but with a different emphasis. All collected gaits require you shorten your reins, an important prerequisite.

Collected Walk At the walk, together with shortening the reins, slightly reduce the "wiping the saddle" motion of your seat. You should be a bit "quieter" and less mobile in your seat as—in the rhythm of the walk—you keep driving the horse forward toward your hands with your seat and legs while you give half-halts to enable you to control the length of steps of the horse's hind legs.

Collected Trot The same applies to the trot. Sit more deeply and restrain with the hand a bit more at the moment you shorten the reins. Increase your driving aids to activate the horse's hind legs. Because of your restraining hand, the active hind legs cannot stride further forward—instead this energy is "converted," so to speak, into more pronounced angling of the joints of the hind legs. This increased flexion in the haunches contributes to them "lowering" (or the horse "sitting down" more) and hence to collection. As soon as the horse gathers his body in this way, you must soften your hands again. The careful orchestration between driving, gathering, and yielding continues, and transforms a common trot into a dance-like movement.

Collected Canter As in the other gaits, collection in the canter is achieved by simply intensifying the aids you already use. This

A collected canter with a lovely uphill tendency and relative elevation.

The Training Pyramid

"As a judge, I can tell from watching every single movement if a horse has been ridden correctly, that is, with the Training Pyramid in mind. Apart from various aspects of form, such as 'arriving at the correct letter' or 'staying on the line,' all dressage tests the individual elements as laid out in the Pyramid. So, in every movement, purity of rhythm is most important, followed by suppleness, contact, impulsion, straightness, and collection. When assessing each movement, I therefore have to find out to what extent these elements have been incorporated into the horse's training. Technical riding inaccuracies (from letter to letter) are less important to me than conceptual mistakes when aspects of the horse's performance are not in accordance with the Training Pyramid."

DR. VOLKER MORITZ
International FEI "O"
dressage judge

means: your outside leg remains behind the girth while you sit slightly deeper in the saddle and shift your weight onto your inside seat bone a little more. Your reins should restrain slightly more than usual at the canter while your seat and legs drive the horse more emphatically toward your hands. This causes the horse to "compress," shorten his stride, lower his haunches, and appear to canter "uphill" with more "jump" through from stride to stride. Softening your hands in response to the development of these qualities is an important aspect of maintaining the collection.

GOAL OF THE MOVEMENT The concept of collection is both an end "goal" in itself, and a "path" for achieving this end goal. It is commonly understood to be at the top of the Training Pyramid, and therefore it is thought to be the pinnacle of what you can achieve through systematic dressage training. Collection—or "self-carriage"—as an end goal is not borne of senseless tradition—its intention is to ultimately keep the horse healthy and sound. When a horse is correctly worked and progressively developed, his ability to eventually collect "rights nature's wrongs," in a sense—collection redistributes the natural weight-bearing system of the horse (majority of weight on the forehand), unburdening the front end and its delicate front legs and hooves and transferring it to the more suitable "engine" in the back (the hindquarters). This redistribution of weight-bearing helps prevent early unsoundness and breakdowns.

Collection is also a part of the path leading to the desirable end result of self-carriage because it's not achieved all of a sudden, with a snap of the fingers, but must be developed in gradual degrees. Progressive work in moderately collected paces, combined with transitions and various other movements, contributes to building the muscle strength necessary for the end goal to be come possible.

FAST FACTS Advanced work; suitable for the work phase of a schooling session; improves strength and endurance.

PYRAMID FACTOR Rhythm*, relaxation/suppleness*, contact*, impulsion**, straightness*, collection.

LEG-YIELDING AWAY FROM AND BACK TO THE TRACK

A forward-and-sideways (lateral) movement at the walk, where the horse, starting on the track, is first ridden toward the center of the arena, then back toward the track.

HOW IT'S SUPPOSED TO LOOK Literally translated from the German as "increasing and decreasing the square," this phrase gives us an idea of how this movement is supposed to look. Picture the entire arena: as you leg-yield (p. 119) from the track toward the centerline, you are effectively "decreasing" the size of the arena. When riding back to the track, you are "increasing" it again.

Similar to a one-loop serpentine (p. 122), this exercise is also away from and back to the track (see diagram, p. 170). Both the leg-yield away from and back to the track is done in a forward-and-sideways movement without lateral bend. Starting from the first letter after the corner on the long side of the arena, ride at an angle to the quarterline, and from there ride back to the letter just before the second corner of the same long side. When you leave the track, flex the horse toward the rail. He should be engaged, move in a distinct rhythmical beat, and travel forward-and-sideways in a diagonal line with the forehand slightly leading. When you arrive at the quarterline (this should happen near or at the middle of the long side), straighten him and ride forward for a horse's length, then change the flexion so the horse is looking toward the center of the arena, and ride back to the track.

MOST COMMON MISTAKES The Horse: labors; hesitates; exhibits little engagement; is tight in the neck; tilts his head at the poll; goes against the rider's hand. **The Rider:** drives the horse too sideways

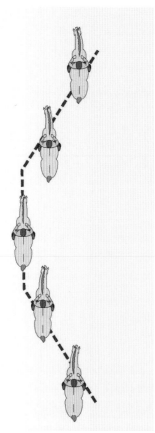

Leg-yielding away from, and back to the track, as viewed from above.

and not enough forward or vice versa; overflexes the neck; plans the pattern poorly; sways with his upper body.

CORRECT AIDS In order to ride this movement successfully, it's important to maintain engagement at the walk and always *first* think forward, *then* sideways. "Thinking" forward helps you avoid the movement turning into a laborious "forcing" of the horse sideways.

When you first come out of the corner and onto the long side of the arena, slightly compress the horse by giving half-halts, then flex him a bit toward the rail. At the same time, slide the new inside leg (the leg "inside" the horse's flex or bend) behind the girth to help drive the horse forward-and-sideways, along with your other leg and seat aids. Alternately drive sideways and drive forward while applying both restraining and yielding aids to keep the horse engaged and moving forward-and-sideways at the walk on the specified diagonal.

On reaching the quarterline (near or at the middle of the long side), straighten the horse and swap the rein and leg aids. This process takes about a horse's length. Once the horse has changed flexion, your new inside leg, now behind the girth in a "guarding" position, pushes the horse forward-and-sideways back toward the track, and the outside leg "absorbs" some of the sideways movement, thus supporting forward impulsion and preventing the horse from *only* moving sideways. When arriving at the track, straighten the horse again, then ride deeply into the corner where you again bend him laterally along his longitudinal axis and flex him to the inside of the arena.

GOAL OF THE MOVEMENT Leg-yielding from and back to the track is a good gymnastic exercise. It activates the horse's inside hind leg, encouraging him to step with it underneath his center of gravity. It also improves straightness, and relaxation and suppleness. Furthermore, the horse learns to be sensitive to the rider's forward-and-sideways driving leg, which is excellent preparation for other lateral movements, such as half-passes (p. 148), later on in training. Because the aids have to be well coordinated, it is an effective exercise for the rider, too.

FAST FACTS Basic exercise; can be ridden at the walk and working trot.

PYRAMID FACTOR Rhythm*, relaxation/suppleness**, contact**, impulsion*, straightness**, collection.

VOLTE
A circular school figure with a diameter of 6, 8, or 10 meters, where the starting and end points are the same.

HOW IT'S SUPPOSED TO LOOK Voltes can be ridden at any given point in the arena. Usually—at least in dressage tests—you are required to ride them starting at a specific arena letter. The size of the volte is also usually specified: they can be 6, 8, or 10 meters in diameter. (Larger voltes are easier to ride than smaller ones.) A volte must be ridden perfectly round, so if you were to "draw" a perpendicular line from the starting point on the track to the center of the arena (see diagram, p. 172), the volte would be halved in two equal portions.

Voltes can be ridden at the walk, trot and canter. The rhythm and beat of the respective gait must be maintained at all times. The horse is flexed and bent around the rider's inside leg according to the line of travel, and the horse's hind legs should follow in the tracks of the front legs.

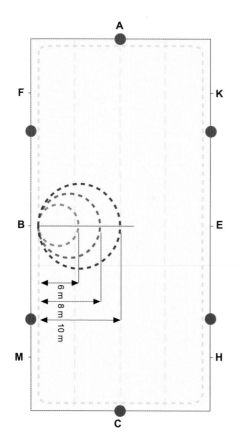

A

F   K

B   E

6 m
8 m
10 m

M   H

C

Voltes always need to be of
equal size on the left and right
side of an imagined
perpendicular line.

MOST COMMON MISTAKES The Horse:
exhibits little or no lateral bend; evades
with his haunches; circles in a travers-like
manner; is tight in the neck; is on the
forehand. **The Rider:** plans the pattern
poorly; doesn't ride the volte perfectly
round; makes the circle too small or too
big; gives the volte "edges" (squares it
off); "pulls" the horse around.

CORRECT AIDS Riding a correct volte
may seem easy, but it is more complicated than you might think. Apart from giving the correct aids and having the right
feel for the movement, you also require
a certain amount of "spatial" sense. For
the rider who is able to imagine his volte
in its precise form in his mind's eye, it's
easier. Here, it also helps to visualize the
quarterlines in the arena in order to ride
voltes in their correct size—at least,
along the long side. Why is this? The
answer is simple: a standard arena is 20 meters wide. To the centerline, it's 10 meters; to the quarterline, 5 meters. So a 10-meter volte is
ridden in its maximum size to the centerline, an 8-meter volte until 2
meters before the centerline, and a 6-meter volte extends 1 meter
beyond the quarterline. Sense of space is just as important in terms
of the "width" of the volte. Here, you really only need to imagine a
perpendicular line running from the point where the volte is begun
to a point 90 degrees to the track (see diagram). The larger the volte,
the more important it is to visualize its size relative to the arena.

To ride a volte, slightly shorten the inside rein and flex the horse in
the poll a few strides before you make your turn onto the circle line.
When you reach the turning point, increase the flexion for the turn

(p. 1), slide your outside leg behind the girth, keep your inside leg positioned at the girth, and bend the horse through his rib cage. Yield the outside rein slightly to allow the horse to stretch his outer neck and torso muscles, and to prevent him from tilting his head at the poll. Maintain enough contact with the outside rein to support the outside leg in keeping the horse's shoulder and hindquarters under control. You must maintain and evenly distribute all these aids until the end of the volte.

Once the horse has taken on the appropriate flexion and bend, your inside hand must now yield to allow his inside hind leg to step forward, guarantee freedom in his shoulder, and help the horse remain balanced. When a horse falls out through his shoulder or moves in a travers-like manner, this is often a sign that your inside rein aid is too strong. Correct the problem by riding in counter-flexion for a stride or two.

GOAL OF THE MOVEMENT Just as transitions (p. 155) promote strength, voltes, too, are excellent gymnastic exercises. A volte combines a variety of components: it shortens, thereby strengthening, the muscles on the inside (neck and body); stretches, thereby suppling, the muscles on the outside; and increases the ability of the joints of the inside haunches to "close" or compress their angles, while increasing the ability of the joints of the outside haunches to "open" or expand.

Since voltes are ridden in both directions, or even with a change of rein, such as in a figure eight (p. 3), they supple the *entire* horse, a prerequisite for straightness, the fifth element in the Training Pyramid. In addition, in a volte a horse is always striving to move more underneath his center of gravity with his inside hind leg, so the exercise improves balance and strength in the hindquarters—thus collection. Incidentally, riding voltes presents the rider with an opportunity to fine-tune his aids, since any mistake he makes will inevitably be immediately obvious. Because of this, the riding of voltes indicates to judges when a horse is ridden correctly or not.

Underestimated

"Voltes are often underestimated. In order to ride them really correctly, the horse must have already been gymnasticized very evenly—on both sides. To ride a really good volte is not that easy. For me, voltes are a measurement of progress: they show how much the horse has been taught in terms of balance and level of training. Before I begin riding voltes, my horse must be able to execute a shoulder-fore. Only then do voltes become part of my training plan. When a rider starts schooling voltes early—especially small circles, it is probably to train the movement itself rather than using the volte as an excellent tool to further all training. Repetition of such a movement at any stage should be avoided, since drilling never assists in a horse's education."

RUDOLF ZEILINGER
Dressage trainer,
Grand Prix rider,
trainer of the Danish dressage team

FAST FACTS Basic exercise; large voltes can be ridden in warm-up, while smaller ones are appropriate in the work phase of a schooling session; voltes at the canter only required from Second Level (Elementary in the UK) onward; improves lateral mobility, builds strength.

PYRAMID FACTOR Rhythm*, relaxation/suppleness**, contact**, impulsion**, straightness**, collection**.

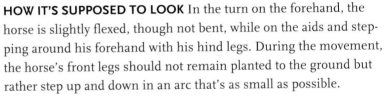

TURN ON THE FOREHAND
A 180-degree turn begun at the halt, where the horse's hindquarters step around his forehand with the front legs remaining more or less in the same spot.

HOW IT'S SUPPOSED TO LOOK In the turn on the forehand, the horse is slightly flexed, though not bent, while on the aids and stepping around his forehand with his hind legs. During the movement, the horse's front legs should not remain planted to the ground but rather step up and down in an arc that's as small as possible.

MOST COMMON MISTAKES The Horse: steps forward; labors; evades backward; evades sideways; goes against the rider's hand; **The Rider:** overflexes the horse; "pulls" the horse around.

In the turn on the forehand the horse's front legs step on the same spot, while his hindquarters make a 180-degree turn around...

CORRECT AIDS A turn on the forehand is not a particularly difficult movement. In order to execute it correctly, however, the horse should first be on the aids and standing evenly on all four legs. Then you slightly flex the horse into the direction of the turn (when on the rail going left, you execute a right turn on the forehand, so flex to the right—toward the rail) while simultaneously applying leg pressure with the leg on the same side (in this case the right leg) behind the girth. This way, you "push" the horse's haunches bit by bit to the side as your restraining rein aids prevent the horse from "escaping" forward. Ask for the turn step-by-step, with the horse stepping around in a controlled manner. To complete the turn on the forehand, straighten the horse again, slide your sideways-driving leg back into its original position at the girth, and using half-halts, bring the horse to a square halt (p. 49) again.

GOAL OF THE MOVEMENT The purpose of the turn on the forehand is to familiarize the horse with the sideways-driving leg aids and to be able to use them at any time. It also provides a practical opportunity to teach the horse to turn in the smallest space possible—not only as may be required in a lower level dressage test but also on a trail ride.

FAST FACTS Basic exercise; improves coordination.

PYRAMID FACTOR Rhythm, relaxation/suppleness, contact*, impulsion, straightness, collection.

ZIGZAG HALF-PASS

A series of forward-and-sideways (lateral) movements, where the horse—flexed and bent in the direction of travel, his body parallel to the long side of the arena—moves with his forehand slightly ahead of his haunches, and his outside legs crossing over his inside legs, and the rider changes direction frequently back and forth, changing the flexion and bend every time she changes direction.

HOW IT'S SUPPOSED TO LOOK Although "zigzag half-pass" describes this movement well, in dressage tests and on score sheets it's not used. There you will find instructions such as, "Down the centerline, three half-passes, 5 meters to either side of the centerline, starting and ending to the right."

Whether ridden at the trot or canter, the half-pass (p. 148) is ridden smoothly forward-and-sideways with the horse's body parallel to the long side of the arena and the forehand always slightly leading the

...and the movement is completed when he is facing the opposite direction.

The half-pass.

hindquarters. When changing direction, fluidity must be maintained with the forehand still always preceding the haunches. Zigzag half-passes should look as if you are unraveling woven material by pulling a loose string—rhythmical, with noticeable cadence, and full of impulsion. The horse should travel away from the line he's on (usually the centerline) equally far to both the left and right.

Zigzag half-passes at the canter can be ridden with a simple change of lead (p. 41) at each change of direction; however, flying changes (p. 45) are commonly required. It's important that you make the change during the moment the horse is straight in *between* the individual half-passes.

MOST COMMON MISTAKES The Horse: leads with his haunches; isn't parallel to the long side; exhibits little lateral bend; loses impulsion; loses rhythm; is tight in the neck; is on the forehand; "throws" his body back and forth in the changes of direction. **The Rider:** asks for too much or too little flexion; loses control of the haunches when changing flexion and bend; rides the incorrect number of strides between changes of direction; plans the pattern poorly; "pulls" the horse around; drives the horse too forward and too little sideways.

CORRECT AIDS The aids for the zigzag half-pass are the same as the regular half-pass: with the inside rein, flex the horse in the direction of travel; your inside leg is at the girth, bending the horse in the rib cage and driving him forward; your outside leg is positioned behind the girth, driving him forward-and-sideways. Your weight shifts onto your inside seat bone, and your shoulders stay "parallel" to the horse's ears.

It is in this position that you approach the point on the line where you plan to switch the direction of the half-pass. Just before this point, decrease the flexion slightly, and when you get to the point of the change, let your inside leg "absorb" the sideways movement as you slide it behind the girth so it becomes the new outside leg. And, at the same time, the other leg (the "new" inside leg), slides forward so it's now at the girth. As this happens, reverse the flexion smoothly, and switch your weight to the new, now inside, seat bone. This shifts the horse's center of gravity, and since the horse always strives to step underneath his center of gravity, he will move into the new direction, supported by your forward-and-sideways driving leg aids and your inside hand lightly guiding him.

Whether you ride this movement at the trot or canter, the aids for the change of direction are the same. At the canter, however, the difficulty lies in riding the change at exactly the right moment. In the beginning, it's important to allow yourself (and your horse) extra time, and ride a canter stride straight ahead before asking him to change to the new direction. This extra stride prevents you from "throwing" the horse back and forth, provoking mistakes. It's also helpful to initiate each change of direction while "thinking shoulder-in"—this will help prevent the haunches from getting out in front of the forehand, incorrectly leading the movement.

In dressage tests, the required number of zigzag half-passes and the distance traveled to the left and right of the centerline are specified. At the trot, distance is outlined in "meters," and at the canter, in "strides." To explain, one meter at the trot is roughly the equivalent of one complete sideways step. If, for instance, a "trot half-pass to the right, 4 meters to the centerline" is required, begin counting as the

In zig-zag half-passes, the horse's legs cross far over— evenly on both sides.

horse's right front leg steps sideways. From then on, only count the right front leg. At the canter, simply count each individual canter stride.

The more changes of direction and half-passes required, the more steeply angled they must be and the more lateral bend they require—all of which increase the level of difficulty.

GOAL OF THE MOVEMENT Zigzag half-passes present a great opportunity for the rider and trainer to test the horse's "through-ness" and suppleness. Only a horse that has been gymnasticized evenly on both reins will be able to oscillate between right and left half-passes as required.

FAST FACTS Advanced movement; ridden in collection only; improves coordination, lateral mobility, and "carrying power."

PYRAMID FACTOR Rhythm*, relaxation/suppleness*, contact*, impulsion*, straightness, collection*.

CIRCLE

A school figure 20 meters in diameter that touches both long sides of the arena, started usually at the letter in the middle of the short side, or occasionally the letter in the middle of the long side—in which case "X" is the center of the circle.

HOW IT'S SUPPOSED TO LOOK Usually, a circle is ridden by start-ing from the short side of the arena. It must be perfectly round and planned so that its four outer points touch the middle of the short side, both circle points on the long sides of the arena (10 meters dis-tance from the short side), and the center at "X." The line of the cir-cle must always be the same distance from its center—you do not ride into the corners of the arena.

Riding circles provides you a variety of additional training movements and exercises, including changing rein out of the circle (p. 22), changing rein through the circle (p. 30), and decreasing and increasing the circle (p. 181). Circles can be ridden in all basic gaits.

MOST COMMON MISTAKES The Rider: does not plan a perfectly round circle; gives the circle "edges" (squares it off); allows the circle to be egg-shaped; does not meet the circle points on the long sides; rides into the corners of the arena.

CORRECT AIDS In order to ride a perfectly round circle, you should have mastered the aids for turning (p. 1), and be able to focus on both the bending line ahead and the four circle points you need to pass through. This means looking ahead toward the next point and *always* turning. To do this, flex the horse to the inside with your inside rein—according to the line of the circle. Keep your inside leg at the girth and slide your outside leg slightly behind the girth to prevent the haunches from evading. These leg aids bend the horse along his longitudinal axis. Yield your outside hand slightly forward to allow the muscles on the horse's outside to stretch; however, maintain enough contact to keep the horse from falling out through his outside shoulder.

When riding in a group, each rider must individually ride toward the points on the circle.

GOAL OF THE MOVEMENT Since it is of generous proportions, the circle is one of the first movements on a bending line that is suitable for a young horse or a horse that's not yet warmed-up. In these cases, the horse should not execute any tight turns that could damage the joints; however, with the circle he can be safely suppled and gently bent to the right and left on his longitudinal axis. Riding circles is a good loosening exercise, and it prepares the horse for tighter turns later on.

Furthermore, if you want to demonstrate a perfect circle, you will need to master the coordination of your rein and leg aids or the circle will not be round as desired. So, the ideal of a neat, round circle is not some futile "invention," but is there to always give information about the overall correctness and effectiveness of the rider's aids.

FAST FACTS Basic exercise; can be ridden in the warm-up in all basic gaits; suitable for the work phase of a schooling session, excepting extended gaits; improves lateral mobility.

PYRAMID FACTOR Rhythm*, relaxation/suppleness**, contact**, impulsion**, straightness**, collection.

DECREASING AND INCREASING THE CIRCLE
Alternately decreasing and increasing the size of a circular school figure.

HOW IT'S SUPPOSED TO LOOK Decreasing and increasing the circle is not a movement required in a dressage test but a gymnastic exercise for daily training. From a regular 20-meter circle (p. 179), the horse spirals in around the circle's center, but to no smaller than the smallest volte (p. 171)—6 meters in diameter. From there, you gradually spiral out again until you reach the original circle line. It's important to always flex and bend the horse evenly, and ride a line accurately around the center of the circle.

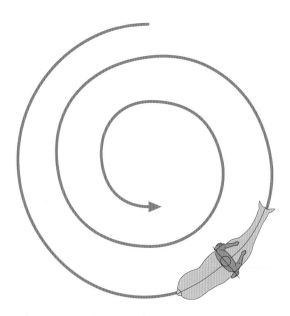

When decreasing the circle, ride the horse in even arcs toward the center of the circle...

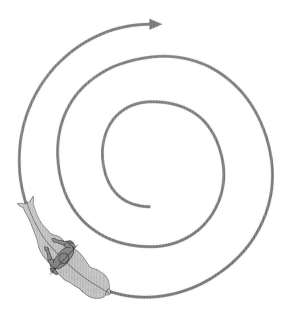

...when increasing the circle, ride out of the circle in the same way.

MOST COMMON MISTAKES The Horse: loses rhythm; evades with the haunches; falls out through the outside shoulder; is tight in the neck; is on the forehand. **The Rider:** overflexes the horse; asks for too little lateral bend; "pulls" the horse around; approaches the center of the circle at an angle (instead of spiraling in); creates an egg-shaped bending line.

CORRECT AIDS When decreasing and increasing the circle, you are really applying a combination of aids used for circles and voltes. During the *decreasing* spiral, flex the horse to the inside with an inside, shortened rein, and bend him around your inside leg at the girth. Slide your outside leg slightly behind the girth to keep the haunches on their track. To achieve an evenly ridden "inward spiral," you need to increase the inside rein aid a bit more, and shift your weight slightly more to the inside seat bone. The inside leg keeps the horse on the desired line and prevents him from "cheating" inward suddenly. When *increasing* the spiral, replace the amplified lateral bend of the decreasing spiral with a "normal" one so the horse can ease his way out of the volte in the center and travel on a spiraling line back out to the original large circle.

GOAL OF THE MOVEMENT Decreasing and increasing the circle at any gait strengthens the horse's inside hind leg, encouraging him to step further underneath his center of gravity. It is a very useful exercise to prepare a horse for collection. Changing the pace within the gait—shortening the stride when decreasing, lengthening it when increasing—strengthens his muscles and promotes impulsion. You can vary the exercise by riding it in shoulder-in-like manner (p. 126) or in a leg-yield (p. 119) at times, one movement following the other, or in other instances alternating it between decreasing and increasing. This way, you can improve the horse's "straightness." And last but not least, circle decreasing and increasing is used as a preliminary stage to the working pirouette (p. 13).

FAST FACTS Basic exercise; can be ridden in the work phase of a schooling session; suitable for working trot and working and collected canter; improves "carrying power" and lateral bend.

PYRAMID FACTOR Rhythm*, relaxation/suppleness**, contact**, impulsion**, straightness**, collection**.

"CHEWING" THE REINS OUT OF THE HANDS
Lengthening the reins—up to a long rein—while maintaining a connection with the horse's mouth.

HOW IT'S SUPPOSED TO LOOK When "chewing" the reins out of the hands, the horse "takes" the reins from you when you offer them: he drops his neck forward-and-downward, to the point where his mouth is at least at the same level with the point of his shoulder. His nose remains in front of the vertical, and his gait, rhythm, and length of stride remain the same.

MOST COMMON MISTAKES The Horse: exhibits contact problems (head tossing, for example); comes off the aids; stretches forward-and-downward only slightly or not all; holds his neck in a "rolled up" position; hurries; runs away; falls onto his forehand; "pokes" his nose downward rather than stretching smoothly; shows inconsistent rhythm. **The Rider:** doesn't give the horse enough rein.

CORRECT AIDS "Chewing" the reins out of the hands is more of an exercise than a real movement, and there are no specific aids for it. Simply open your fists a bit so the horse can "take" the reins from you and stretch forward-and-downward. Depending on the gait, all necessary aids should simply continue.

A horse that has not been worked consistently "over his back" often reveals problems during this exercise; he won't want (and probably is not able) to stretch toward your hand in the required manner. When this happens, it can help to ride the horse in position (p. 142) on a long rein for several strides. Increasing lateral bend while driving the horse forward at the same time helps most horses step better into your hand and be more inclined to stretch their neck.

With a horse that tends to hurry, initially do this exercise at the rising trot (p. 77) on a circle, and rise the trot "against" the rhythm of the horse. How do you do this? It's quite simple: when rising, remain standing for a longer moment before sitting back down in the saddle. This will feel quite awful—for you *and* the horse! Most horses respond by being a little irritated, and attempt to adjust to the change in the rider's seat by slowing down.

When "chewing" the reins out of the hands, the horse should stretch forward and downward toward the rider's hand—as shown. In this photo, the horse's nose could be slightly more forward.

GOAL OF THE MOVEMENT This exercise gives an excellent indication, at any time in training, as to whether or not a horse and rider are performing with good and correct basics. Mistakes that occur quickly reveal fundamental deficiencies in training, especially in the areas of rhythm, contact, and relaxation and suppleness—the first three elements of the Training Pyramid. For instance, a horse that has been forced into a certain frame with strong rein influence, force, or artificial means, will never correctly "chew" the reins out of the hands. For this reason, in dressage tests, it is used by judges to expose hidden problems. It should be part of your daily work regimen since it allows you to evaluate whether your training is progressing correctly. Only a horse that's well ridden will trustingly stretch into a long rein while maintaining the same gait and rhythm—and will do so at any given time.

FAST FACTS Basic exercise; rider can perform it at any given time as a "progress check."

PYRAMID FACTOR Rhythm*, relaxation/suppleness**, contact**, impulsion*, straightness, collection.

INCREASING PACE
Increasing the length of stride at the trot or canter while maintaining essentially the same tempo.

HOW IT'S SUPPOSED TO LOOK Increasing the pace in the trot or canter is not a movement; it simply describes a process that is a preliminary stage to lengthening of stride movements: medium trot (p. 85), medium canter (p. 89), extended trot, and extended canter (p. 134). The horse's strides should become bigger and longer, covering more ground, caused by an increase in thrust from the hindquarters. The horse should always show an "uphill" tendency and elongate his frame.

MOST COMMON MISTAKES The Horse: "runs"; hurries; covers little ground; exhibits little impulsion; is on the forehand; strides wide behind; shows little suspension ("flat"); gets "tight" or tense.

CORRECT AIDS In order to increase the pace, you must get the horse's attention by giving a half-halt—that is, "compress" his body a bit more by using your seat, legs, and reins. This creates extra energy, which can then be released in a controlled manner in the form of more forward thrust if the rider moves his hands slightly forward at the moment of increasing the pace, and continues to drive the horse forward using his seat and both legs at the girth.

GOAL OF THE MOVEMENT In a riding lesson, a familiar instruction might be to "Increase the pace on the next long side." This doesn't really tell you if you are expected to lengthen stride (p. 153), ride a medium trot or canter, or even an extended gait. During training, however, this isn't so important since increasing the pace is a useful exercise in itself, regardless in what form it is ridden.

In any type of increase in pace, the horse's frame should lengthen, as the author is showing here.

Elongating the frame while increasing thrust not only activates new muscle groups, it also contributes to furthering the horse's overall suppleness. Alternating between increasing and decreasing the pace is therefore an important exercise, which—when made part of daily training—contributes to developing and strengthening muscles in the haunches.

FAST FACTS Basic exercise; can be ridden in the warm-up and in the work phase of a schooling session; intended for trot and canter; improves "pushing power."

PYRAMID FACTOR Rhythm**, relaxation/suppleness**, contact**, impulsion**, straightness*, collection.

RESOURCES

United States Dressage Federation (USDF)

4051 Iron Works Parkway

Lexington, KY 40511

USA

Fax: 1 859 971 7722

Tel: 1 859 971 2277

www.usdf.org

British Dressage

Stoneleigh Park

Kenilworth

Warwickshire

CV8 2RJ

ENGLAND

Fax: +44 024 76 690390

Tel: +44 024 76 69830

E-mail: office@britishdressage.co.uk

www.britishdressage.co.uk

German Equestrian Federation (FN)

Deutsche Reiterliche Vereinigung e.V.

Bundesverband für Pferdesport und Pferdezucht

Fédération Equestre Nationale (FN)

Freiherr-von-Langen-Straße 13

48231 Warendorf

GERMANY

Fax: +49 02581 62144

Tel: +49 02581 6362-0

www.pferd-aktuell.de

Fédération Equestre International (FEI)

Avenue Mon Repos 24

1005 Lausanne

SWITZERLAND

Fax: +41 21 310 47 60

Tel: +41 21 310 47 47

www.fei.org

PHOTOS AND ILLUSTRATION CREDITS

All photos by Alois Müller except:

Lothar Lenz/Kosmos (pp. 8, 12, 17, 50, 56, 64, 88, 93, 154, 157, 164)

mawe-Bilderdienst (p. 186)

Julia Rau/Kosmos (pp. 7, 71, 156)

Christof Salata/Kosmos (p. 180)

Barbara Schnell (pp. 29, 86, 88, 93, 139, 149, 188)

Illustrations by Cornelia Koller

RECOMMENDED READING

Ride Horses with Awareness and Feel
The New Dressage Training System
from the Dutch Olympians at Academy Bartels
TINEKE & JOEP BARTELS
168 pp, 103 color photos

Tug of War: Classical versus "Modern" Dressage
Why Classical Training Works and How Incorrect "Modern" Riding
Negatively Affects Horses' Health
DR. GERD HEUSCHMANN
144 pp, 76 color photos, 20 illustrations

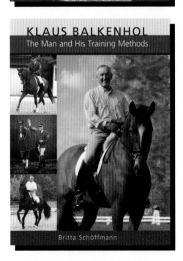

Klaus Balkenhol
The Man and His Training Methods
BRITTA SCHÖFFMANN
160 pp, 175 color photos